LETTERS FROM THE DESERT

ST VLADIMIR'S SEMINARY PRESS
Popular Patristics Series
Number 26

The Popular Patristics Series published by St Vladimir's Seminary Press provides readable and accurate translations of a wide range of early Christian literature to a wide audience—students of Christian history to lay Christians reading for spiritual benefit. Recognized scholars in their fields provide short but comprehensive and clear introductions to the material. The texts include classics of Christian literature, thematic volumes, collections of homilies, letters on spiritual counsel, and poetical works from a variety of geographical contexts and historical backgrounds. The mission of the series is to mine the riches of the early Church and to make these treasures available to all.

Series Editor
JOHN BEHR

Associate Editor
AUGUSTINE CASIDAY

Letters
from the
Desert

BARSANUPHIUS AND JOHN

A Selection of Questions and Responses

Translation and Introduction by

JOHN CHRYSSAVGIS

ST VLADIMIR'S SEMINARY PRESS
CRESTWOOD, NEW YORK 10707

Library of Congress Cataloging-in-Publication Data

Barsanuphius, Saint, 6th cent.
[Biblos psychophelestate periechousa apokriseis. English]
Letters from the desert : a selection of questions and responses /
Barsanuphius and John : translation and introduction by John Chryssavgis.
    p.   cm. — (St. Vladimir's Seminary Press popular patristics series)
Includes bibliographical references (p.) and index.
ISBN 0–88141–254–6
    1. Asceticism—History—Early church, ca. 30–600.   I. John, the Prophet,
Saint.   II. Chryssavgis, John.   III. Title.   IV. Series.

BR60.B3713 2003
275.694'02—dc21

                                                                    2003049823

COPYRIGHT © 2003
ST VLADIMIR'S SEMINARY PRESS
575 Scarsdale Rd., Crestwood, NY 10707
1-800-204-2665
www.svspress.com

ISBN 978–0–88141–254–3
ISSN 1555–5755

PRINTED IN THE UNITED STATES OF AMERICA

Table of Contents

Barsanuphius and John:
The Old Men of Gaza

An Introduction to their *Letters*, Teaching and World

> "I regard myself as *a slave on a mission*"
> (*Letter* 139)

With the above statement, the Great Old Man (or Elder), Barsanuphius, responds to a request for prayers. He considers himself as a "slave" with a particular mission or commission. Indeed, in another response, he calls the Other Old Man, John, his "fellow-slave" (*Letter* 186). This phrase is a definition of his identity as marked by a sense of enslavement to the inspiration of God and a sense of obligation to the tradition of the past. At the same time, however, the phrase defines his own embodiment of that tradition in all that he is and does, as well as his articulation and communication of the same tradition in conversation with and counsel toward his disciples.

This is the conviction with which these elders offer a "spiritual word of counsel" with the assurance that their disciples are in fact receiving "the healing medicine of the word of the Spirit" (*Letter* 570c). In their minds and in their words, the authority of God is at stake as they advise their disciples on practical and spiritual matters. Throughout this correspondence, the elders are affirming and defending the authority of the divine Word.

INTRODUCTION

Christian Palestine enjoyed centuries of prominence in Hellenistic and Roman times, owing to its privileged status and strategic situation—in terms of geography, climate, and history. A major commercial area from biblical times, this southern coastal region was always coveted territory throughout history. For the adherents of the Christian Scriptures, the Apostle Philip evangelized the Ethiopian eunuch on the way to Gaza (Acts 8.26).

The Ethiopian was not the only person to be touched, even converted, by the region. The Gaza region proved a remarkable place of welcome and continuity for Christian monasticism toward the end of the fourth century. Its accessibility by sea and road, its proximity to Egypt and Syria as well as to the Holy Land itself, rendered Gaza a critical haven for particular expressions that offered fresh perspectives in the spiritual and intellectual tradition of the monastic phenomenon.

Christian emperors, numerous pilgrims, and monastic developments; the deserts, rivers, and sand dunes; the roads, the literature, as well as the renowned produce of spices and wines—all of these were to play a critical role in the formation of this unique area. Travelers journeyed from Palestine to Egypt in order to visit the elders of the Egyptian desert.[1] From as early as the mid-fourth century, some of the better-known pilgrims included Jerome and Rufinus, Palladius and Evagrius, as well as John Cassian, who later translated the desert tradition of Egypt to the West.

At the end of the same century, another movement began in the opposite direction, namely from Egypt to Palestine. Monastics fled the renowned wilderness, bringing with them their practices and teachings. The primary causes of this emigration included *internal*

---

[1] *Letters* 30–31 of our correspondence, exchanged between Barsanuphius and John of Beersheba, recall a journey by boat made by the latter to Egypt. I am grateful to Dr Jennifer Hevelone Harper for her insightful and invaluable comments on this introduction and the translation that follows.

factors, such as the condemnation of Origenism by Theophilus of Alexandria in 400, as well as *external fears*, such as the threat of raiding desert tribes. Three hundred monks—many of these educated and cultivated—left Egypt definitively for Sinai, Jerusalem, and the region around the Dead Sea, some of them even traveling as far as Asia Minor.

PALESTINIAN MONASTICISM

Palestine is divided into two distinct monastic regions. The first of these is centered around the Holy City, also including the territory around Jerusalem and as far as the Dead Sea; the second lies in the southern region around Gaza. It is in the latter region that our two elders, Barsanuphius and John, flourished in the early part of the sixth century.

Monastics in Palestine were generally well aware of their *biblical roots*. Barsanuphius is convinced that "God revealed the way of life through the prophets and the apostles" (*Letter* 605). This was, after all, the land where the prophets once wandered, the desert where Jesus had prayed and fasted, the soil where the seeds of the Church were first planted.

Furthermore, monastics of Palestine were also characterized by a keen memory of the *martyrs and confessors*. Barsanuphius would draw connections between the monk and the martyr: "To renounce one's proper will is a sacrifice of blood. It means that one has reached the point of laboring unto death and of ignoring one's own will" (*Letter* 254).

Finally, monks in the surrounding areas of Gaza were abundantly familiar with *earlier ascetic figures*, with monastic developments and particular lifestyles that had preceded them, especially admitting their indebtedness to the Desert Fathers and Mothers of Egypt. One will, for instance, frequently read in the *Letters* of Barsanuphius and John the following kind of references to these fathers:

We have also seen in the ancient fathers such an example
(*Letter* 60)

The fathers have said (*Letter* 86)

This is the way of the fathers (*Letter* 212)

Let us speak those things, which contribute to edification,
from the *Sayings of the Fathers* (*Letter* 469).

The history of the region is rich in monastic figures and founders.
Hilarion (c. 292–c. 372) lived for almost twenty of his earlier years in
this region. Born in Thavatha, some five miles south of Gaza, he was
schooled in Alexandria. During his time there, he also met Antony
the Great, the Father of Monasticism. Upon returning to his native
Palestine, Hilarion assumed a small cell near the port of Maiouma,
where he also received numerous visitors for counsel.

Another well-known monk and monastic author in this region
was Abba Isaiah of Scetis. A later emigrant from Egypt, Isaiah had
spent many years in a monastery as well as in the desert of Scetis. He
moved to Palestine, fleeing fame, between 431 and 451. He first set-
tled near Eleftheropolis, moving finally to Beit Daltha near Gaza,
only some four miles from Thavatha, which was already known as
the birthplace of Hilarion and which later was to become familiar as
the site of the monastery of Abba Seridos.[2] Indeed, Gaza and its
environs will be indelibly marked by the presence of the two remarkable elders of the next century, Barsanuphius and John.

BARSANUPHIUS AND JOHN

We do not know exactly when Barsanuphius, himself an Egyptian
monk, entered the hilly region of Thavatha (*Letter* 61) and chose to

[2]More on Abba Isaiah in J. Chryssavgis and P.R. Penkett, *Abba Isaiah of Scetis:
Ascetic Discourses* (Kalamazoo, MI: Cistercian Publications, 2002).

lead the enclosed life of a recluse in a nearby cell. From this position, he offered counsel to a number of ascetics who were gradually attracted around the Old Man as he developed a reputation for discernment and compassion.

One of these monks, Abba Seridos, who also attended to Barsanuphius, was presumably appointed Abbot of a monastic community created precisely in order to organize the increasing number of monks that gradually gathered around Barsanuphius. This Seridos was the only person permitted to communicate with Barsanuphius, acting as a mediator for those who wished to submit questions in writing and who expected to receive a similar response through the same avenue.

This monastery became the center of attraction for many monastics and visitors during the sixth century, largely due to the presence in the region of the two Old Men, but partly also due to its activities, which included various workshops (*Letters* 553–554), two guest-houses (*Letters* 570, 595–596), a hospital (*Letters* 327 and 548), and a large church (*Letter* 570).

Barsanuphius, himself a Copt, explains how, as an ascetic rule, he had determined that he should not write by his own hand, but only and always by way of Seridos:

> *Question* (no. 55). A certain elderly Egyptian man . . . asked whether it would be possible to be allowed to meet him.

> *The holy Old Man wrote his response in Greek, as follows:*

> Since I have promised myself not to write to anyone directly, but only to respond through the Abbot, this is why I have not written to you in Egyptian as you wrote to me, but was compelled to tell him to write to you in Greek. For, he does not know Egyptian. . . .

> If I open to you, then I open to all; and if I do not open to you, nor do I have to open to anyone else.

Since Seridos did not know Coptic, he would write in Greek. He was probably Greek, although he may also possibly have been Syrian. The correspondence in fact offers more information about the Abbot Seridos than about the two main elders (see especially *Letter* 570).

Some time between 525 and 527, another hermit, named John, came to live beside Barsanuphius, who surrendered his own cell to him, while he moved to a nearby new cell that he constructed. It is at this point that Barsanuphius becomes known—in the correspondence itself and in posterity—as "the holy Old Man" or "the Great Old Man," Coptic phrases that were familiar among Egyptian circles, and ascribed also by Palladius to Antony. John is called "the Prophet" (*Letters* 785–789) or simply known as "the Other Old Man." The two shared the same way of life and supported one another's ministry (*Letters* 224–225 and 571–572). John assumed another monk—Dorotheus of Gaza—as a disciple, attendant and mouthpiece, for at least part of the next eighteen years that John was the colleague of Barsanuphius.

We know very little about the early years of Barsanuphius. *Letters* 74 and 512 reveal that he was often ill, while *Letters* 13 and 258 admit his temptations of the flesh in his youth. He ate three loaves of bread a week (*Letters* 72 and 97), but we are also told that perhaps he did not have to eat at all (*Letter* 78). He was recognized for his humility (*Letter* 192), discernment (*Letter* 170), foresight (*Letters* 1, 27, 31, 54, 163, and 800), love (*Letters* 110 and 17), illumination (*Letter* 10), and the sharing of his gifts with others (*Letters* 10, 111, and 212). He forgave sins (for example, *Letters* 10, 145, 147, 212, 235, and 166) and even assumed upon himself the sins of others (*Letters* 59 and 235).[3] He was even known for certain miracles worked through his prayers (*Letters* 1, 43, 47, 171, 174, 227, 510, and 581). Generosity and graciousness are characteristic features of Barsanuphius. He offers of his own and of himself. To those who approach him,

---

[3]Barsanuphius forgives sins, although we are unaware of whether he was ordained. John is clearly not ordained (*Letters* 44 and 138).

he conveys a word of advice, he gladly gives a word of prayer, he grants some bread or a piece of clothing (see *Letters* 1, 63, 166, 173, and others).

We know still less about the life of the Other Old Man, John. What we do know is that, while John stayed for the most part in the shadow of Barsanuphius, as his disciple (*Letter* 130), the latter nonetheless claimed that John held the same authority as his master (*Letter* 188).

The authority of John may be described as *more institutional*, responding as he does to problems of a practical nature; the authority of Barsanuphius is *more inspirational*, responding to principles of a spiritual nature. Yet, they do not compete against one another; rather, they appear to complement each other's work. Together, they maintain the integrity of an authority-in-charity. In this respect, the authority that they share is derived from the fact that they also share the same God (*Letter* 20) and the same virtue (*Letter* 780). Consequently, they support one another's ministry.

> *Response* (no. 305). If all of us are one (Jn 17.21)—the Old Man in God and I in the Old Man—then I dare to say that, if he gave you his word, I too give you mine through him. I know that I am weak and the least; yet, I cannot separate myself from the Old Man. For he is compassionate on me so that the two of us are one. . . .

The authority exercised by these elders is truly remarkable and nothing less than refreshing. At a time when monastic life in the West appeared increasingly to become regulated and even codified, in accordance to Roman legal norms and forms, Palestinian monasticism still preserved the flexibility and fluidity of the earlier Egyptian lifestyles. The emphasis in Western monasticism was gradually being focused on discipline; yet, Eastern monasticism always seemed to retain an emphasis on discernment. Spiritual direction in the Christian East was always more personal, significantly less institutional.

In the West, at least increasingly so, one became attached to a community or, in later centuries, selected an Order; in the East, one sought out an elder, an Old Man (*geron* in the Greek; or *abba*, the Coptic word). Indeed, the chief social role of monastic centers in the East through the centuries was to provide spiritual directors; the deeper expectation when one entered a monastery was that one would discover men or women of prayer, not learned scholars or committed missionaries.[4]

Curiously, then, the "invisibility" of Barsanuphius and John became the very reasons for their accessibility and eminence. These elders acted as an alternative source of authority, independent of and beyond the civic and ecclesiastical leadership of their time. The relationship between bishops and monks was never straightforward in history.[5] Yet, inasmuch as never formally resolved, it often proved to be a creative tension in the Christian Church. In fact, Barsanuphius even grants John the specific responsibility and role of directing bishops (*Letters* 788–789). The connection, then, between monks and hierarchs existed, albeit strained. Bishops submitted to the counsel of holy elders (see *Letters* 794–801)—although not always, and not always willingly. Elders refrained from publicly challenging Church hierarchy (*Letter* 792)—although not always, and not always happily.

As already mentioned, the Other Old Man bears the additional title of "Prophet," a reflection and recognition of his spiritual discernment.[6] Before him, Abba Zeno had also been called "the Prophet," while Abba Isaiah of Scetis was described as "the third

[4]On aspects of spiritual direction, see J. Chryssavgis, *Soul Mending: The Art of Spiritual Direction* (Boston: Holy Cross Press, 2000). On the unique relationship between the two elders and their disciples, see also the unpublished doctoral dissertation by J.L. Hevelone-Harper, *Letters to the Great Old Man: monks, laity, and spiritual authority in sixth-century Gaza* (Princeton University, 2000), especially 139–157.

[5]Cf. P. Brown, *Power and Persuasion in Late Antiquity* (University of Wisconsin Press: 1992). Also see H. Chadwick, "Bishops and Monks," in *Studia Patristica* 24 (1993): 45–61, and J. Meyendorff, "St Basil, Messalianism and Byzantine Christianity," *St Vladimir's Theological Quarterly* 24, 4 (1980): 219–234.

[6]See the *Life of Dositheus*, who was the disciple of Dorotheus, ch. I, 6–8, p. 122 in P. M. Brun, *La Vie de Saint Dosithée*, in *Orientalia Christiana Periodica* 26 (Rome,

Prophet Isaiah." The Other Old Man foretold but delayed his death, as we are informed in *Letter* 224, at the request of Aelianos, the successor of Seridos as Abbot of the community, in order to respond to questions by Aelianos relating to the administration of the monastery. The Other Old Man also had the gifts of foresight (*Letter* 777) and tears (*Letter* 565), of discernment (*Letter* 805) and miracles (*Letter* 781).

Nonetheless, sensational miracles and exceptional charismata are neither the most striking nor the most appealing feature of these elders. They did not provide wisdom on request; nor did they attempt to solve all problems presented before them. Their purpose was to inspire rather than to impress; their aim was to exhort rather than to excite. Most of the time, their counsel is practical: one should simply do one's best (*Letter* 302). Their advice is balanced: in everything that one does, one should never hurt one's neighbor (*Letter* 26). They sought to encourage and enable their spiritual directees by gently guiding them on the way that they had already undertaken, rather than discouraging them by austerely correcting or abruptly diverting them from that path.

In his *Historia Ecclesiastica*, Evagrius dedicates an entire chapter to Barsanuphius, noting that, at the time of his own writing, namely around 593, some fifty years after Barsanuphius' death, the Great Old Man was still believed to be living. Although no one had ever seen the Old Man or brought him food, yet the popular belief was that he had not died. The Patriarch of Jerusalem ordered that the door of the cell be opened and a consuming fire is said to have flashed out of the cell, causing all those present to flee![7] Whether in life or in death, Barsanuphius sought to remain unseen. His way and teaching, however, would not remain concealed. Barsanuphius and John are remembered on February 6 in the Eastern calendar.

1932) and reviewed by F. Halkin in *Analecta Bollandiana* 52 (1935): 413–15. Also appeared in *Sources Chrétiennes* 92 (Paris: Cerf, 1952), 122–45.

[7] See Evagrius, *Historia Ecclesiastica* IV, 33 in PG 87. ii: 2764 and S. Vailhé, "Saint Barsanuphe," *Echos d'Orient* 8 (1905): 16.

DISCIPLES OF THE ELDERS: JOHN OF BEERSHEBA,
DOROTHEUS OF GAZA, SERIDOS THE ABBOT AND
AELIANOS

The opening letters of the correspondence are from John of Beersheba and reveal a pious monk hailing from Beersheba. Were it not for *Letter* 3, addressed by the "Other Old Man" to John of Beersheba, and for a reference in *Letter* 9 wherein Barsanuphius forwards greetings from himself, Seridos, and "our brother John," it would be very easy—and surely very tempting—to identify the Other Old Man with the John of Beersheba who is the recipient of the early letters of the correspondence. In addition, *Letter* 13 indicates that Seridos is acquainted with "three [presumably distinct] persons," namely Barsanuphius, John the Prophet, and John of Beersheba.

It is generally assumed that John was well known as an anchorite in Beersheba but later chose to live in the community of Seridos under the spiritual guidance of Barsanuphius. Perhaps he was attracted by the fluidity of the monastic brotherhood administered by Seridos. Barsanuphius, after all, sometimes communicated individually—albeit always through Seridos—with several monks of the monastery itself (*Letters* 250 and 503). That John was not originally a member of the Seridos community is quite apparent from the opening question of the correspondence. Yet, at the same time, Barsanuphius speaks to John with a tone of familiarity from the outset of his epistolary relationship with him. Barsanuphius permits John to assume a semi-eremitic life within the confines of the monastery (*Letter* 32). With time, however, Barsanuphius accepts John to adopt the solitary life (*Letter* 36), even allowing him to assume the responsibility of directing others spiritually (*Letters* 37–43).

The type of paternal direction promoted by Barsanuphius in his letters and fostered among the monks of his nearby community could not but reveal tensions and problems. There are revealing letters dealing with problems that arose between elders and their disciples (*Letters* 489–491 and 503–504). Presented here for posterity are the practical results of *an open structure of spiritual authority and personal guidance.* Yet, this formation is more aptly described as a dynamic process rather than as an established system. It is a tentative and delicate structure, still very much in ongoing development. Barsanuphius and John thought and acted in terms of process and progress. Both elders sought constantly to encourage the freedom of the brothers; if he chastised the deacon who rebelled against his Abbot (*Letter* 239), this surely indicates the spiritual space enjoyed by the brothers as well as the possibility to do precisely that.

Perhaps the best known among the disciples of the two elders is Dorotheus of Gaza. Dorotheus was intimately associated with all three key figures of the community in Thavatha: Barsanuphius, John, and Seridos. An aristocrat, intelligent and well educated, Dorotheus is characterized by a sensitivity in regard to his brothers.

Several letters between *Letters* 570 and 599 present us with information about the lives of John, Seridos, and Aelianos—the successor to Seridos as Abbot of the monastery. At some point in time, however, between 543 and 544, the monastery underwent several significant changes: Abbot Seridos died, and the Other Old Man, John, followed suit very soon after (*Letter* 576); Barsanuphius entered a life of complete seclusion, thereafter practicing total silence in a sealed cell; and Dorotheus decided to leave that community.

Around one hundred questions are addressed by Dorotheus (*Letters* 252–338, and certain others), taking readers through an entire biographical and spiritual exposition of the inner life of this exceptional novice and then monk, later possibly also Abbot of his own monastery and himself author of influential teachings. Dorotheus of Gaza is perhaps even better known to more recent readers than his own spiritual masters. This is possibly due to the fact that the Jesuits, and the West in general, early discovered his writings, which also appear—at length, though not in full—in *Patrologia Graeca* volume 88 (cols. 1611–1844). The first generations of Jesuits were considerably influenced by Dorotheus, recommending his teaching to their novices as preparation for entry into the Society of Jesus.[8]

A series of twenty-nine letters (571–598) describes the dramatic adjustments as spiritual authority changed hands in the monastery. For several decades, Barsanuphius and John had directed the illustrious community at Thavatha. Seridos had left behind a will, which included a list of monks who might replace him. We are informed that all other candidates declined out of humility (*Letter* 574). Finally, a layman (*Letter* 574), Aelianos, was appointed to lead the monastery, after first being tonsured monk, ordained priest, and installed as Abbot (*Letter* 575). Aelianos was a wealthy man (*Letter* 571), himself also previously in correspondence and contact with the two elders of Gaza about the possibility of retirement to the community.

THE LETTERS: "QUESTIONS" AND "ANSWERS"

The correspondence begins with fifty-four questions to and responses by Barsanuphius, with the exception of one letter written by the Other Old Man (*Letter* 3). These opening letters are a series of queries addressed by John of Beersheba, inquiring anxiously about his gradual transition to the eremitic life in Thavatha.

Toward the end of the first letter, Abba Seridos expresses concern about whether he could remember all that Barsanuphius told him in response to the opening question by John of Beersheba. He regrets not having recorded the words of the Old Man in dictation. Barsanuphius comforts him, assuring him that the Holy Spirit would enable him to remember what was said. Indeed, the correspondence continues, with Seridos now prepared for what was to come.

In all, there are—depending on the division adopted for some of the longer documents—approximately eight hundred and fifty

[8]See the articles on Dorotheus of Gaza by L. Regnault in *Dictionnaire de Spiritualité* and, at greater length, in *Revue d' Ascétique et de Mystique* 130 (April–June 1957): 141–49.

letters, dictated by both of our elders, in response to a variety of issues presented by a diverse group of questioners. Almost four hundred letters—including most of the longer ones—are dictated by Barsanuphius; around four hundred and fifty letters are attributed to John. Some letters are not clearly attributed to either of the elders. Moreover, the collection does not contain the entire correspondence.

While the study, and indeed the literature, of spiritual direction has traditionally focused on monastic development, the correspondence of Barsanuphius and John redresses a balance in this regard, concentrating much of its attention on the concerns of laypersons as well. The recipients of these letters include monks from the monastery of Abba Seridos and simple laypersons[9] from the surrounding community, through to high-ranking political officials and even ecclesiastical leaders.

Every question, and indeed every detail of every question, is considered as important and deserving of a response. John reassures a disciple: "Brother, in his responses to you, the Old Man left no question unanswered" (*Letter* 306). The *written means* of communication favored such a *more comprehensive* answer, while the *dual ministry* of the elders provided a *more complete* response to the questions and requests made through the scribe (*Letter* 783). Sometimes, the disciple would be advised to search for a second opinion (*Letters* 361 and 504) or even—on one occasion—to search for the answers within himself, rather than depending on another person outside of himself: "Do not seek answers from anyone in regard to yourself, but create the answers for yourself" (*Letter* 347b). On other occasions, the silence of the elders appears to be the only fitting and healing response (*Letter* 148).

The letters are wide-ranging not only in terms of their recipients, but equally so in regard to their requests. People ask about ordinary circumstances of everyday life. The letters touch on such subjects as

[9]While there are no letters from women in the correspondence, Barsanuphius is not exclusive in his attitude toward women (*Letter* 61). Moreover, the community at Thavatha welcomed female visitors (*Letter* 595) for instruction.

the interpretation of dreams, conduct toward slaves, social relations with non-Christians, Jews and pagans alike (*Letters* 686, 732–735, 776–777, 836, and 821–822), as well as coping with illness (*Letters* 637–646, 753–755, and 778–781). They reveal a diverse community around sixth-century Gaza, with Christians seeking direction about relations with Jews, pagans, and heretics.[10]

The counsel of the elders is always moderate and mild (*Letter* 26). Laypeople inquire about illness and healing; the elders encourage them to consider the importance of spiritual health (Letters 637–644, 753–755, and 778–781; see also *Letters* 72–123 to a monk in illness). Other questions relate to legal and economic matters (*Letters* 667–672, and 749–756), to family relations and chores (*Letters* 764–768), to marriage and death (*Letters* 646 and 676), to property and charity (*Letters* 617–620, 623, 625–626, 629–635, 649), to the proper interaction and appropriate boundaries between monks and laity (*Letters* 636, 681–682, 712–718, 727–729, 736–742, and 751), to the practice of ascetic ways in city life (*Letters* 764–774), and to the importance of superstitions and visions (*Letters* 44 and 414–419).

A monk of the nearby community originally compiled and edited these letters. The editor recorded the correspondence, introducing each letter, occasionally naming the correspondent, and briefly describing the context or defining the purpose of the question addressed to the elders. Sometimes the question is quoted in full; at other times, it is summarized in brief. We are not illumined about the identity of the editor. He does, however, inform readers that he was present, on one occasion, when one visitor wondered whether Barsanuphius was a real person at all; the Great Old Man came out and washed the feet of the doubting visitor in order to allay his suspicions, returning to his cell without speaking a word (*Letter* 125).

These letters are not, and were never intended, to constitute any kind of monastic "rule." The letters of Barsanuphius and John are

[10]After Justinian's decree against pagans in 528–529, for instance, relations between Christians and pagans grew tense and confused, sometimes even violent.

very personal in both style and content. The *Prologue* that opens the text, clearly authored by the editor of the correspondence, states clearly:

> The same teachings are not suited to all alike. . . . Therefore, we must not receive as a general rule the words spoken in a loving way to particular people for the sake of their weakness; rather, we should immediately discern that the response was surely addressed by the saints to the questioner in a personal way.

The letters, indeed, refer not to monastic rules[11] but to spiritual stages. They describe the entire spectrum of the spiritual life, all of the shades and "stages" of the ascetic way (see *Letter* 1). These stages are not random, but developmental; and the "two elders" are able to recognize the various gradations within each stage, as well as the integration of them all.

Although the letters are not organized into any definite order, with the first efforts to do so occurring as late as the fourteenth century, a general summary or division of the letters may be presented in the following scheme:

1. *Letters* 1–224: responses predominantly to hermits about the way of silence.

2. *Letters* 225–616: responses mostly to various brothers of the monastic community headed by Seridos, and especially to questions addressed by Dorotheus.

3. *Letters* 617–850: responses primarily to laypeople and other leaders in the Church and society.

---

[11]The letters (571–598) addressed to Aelianos, the future Abbot of the monastery of Abba Seridos, present some insights into how a monastery should be constituted and administered. However, even in this case, the letters offer general spiritual direction, not practical managerial prescriptions or precise administrative directives.

The letters themselves are sometimes very brief (for example, *Letter* 437), while at other times much longer (for instance, *Letter* 256), to the point of even constituting entire educational treatises (such as *Letter* 604).

Nevertheless, perhaps the most immediate and striking feature of the letters is their spontaneity and freshness, as well as their monastic shrewdness and even their inimitable sense of humor. Not only are the "authors" themselves characterized by a sense of authenticity and originality, but their correspondence is neither a systematic treatise on the spiritual life, nor a document carefully prepared for publication. The correspondence is *a text of a particular time*, albeit with far-reaching influence on spiritual readers through the centuries on account of its wit and wisdom.

It is, moreover, *a text of a particular place*, albeit with far-reaching impact on a variety of cultures on account of its spiritual and pastoral depth. Most of the questions are addressed by visitors, who come to the monastery from the region of Gaza, from the town of Thavatha, or the city of Gaza specifically, and from Palestine generally: hermits, monks in communities, deacons, priests, bishops, lay people, soldiers, teachers, officials, and spouses. They explore the daily life and problems encountered in their particular vocations, in their families, in their communities, in their neighborhoods, in their churches, in their society.

The style of the language adopted in the correspondence is also deeply personal, and for this reason very powerful. While the correspondence comprises around 850 letters, in actual fact we should envisage these letters in the context of personal visitations to the two Old Men. Therefore, in the opening sections of the correspondence, some of the letters will begin with the phrase: "*Write to* [so and so] . . ." (for instance, *Letters* 1, 4, 6, 8–9, 16, 22, 27, and 31). Nevertheless, at the same time, others will replace the word "write" with the word "*say* [or, tell] so and so" and thus begin: "Tell brother [so and so] . . ." (for instance, *Letters* 2–3, 7, 12–15, 19, 26–30, 39, 42, 47, and 54).

The context of the letters is clearly one of familiarity between master and disciple (see *Letters* 56, 62, 68–69, 72–74, 86, 90–93, 96–98, and 126). Moreover, it is reminiscent of the relationship between father/mother and child that forms the basis of monastic life in fourth-century Egypt. The words frequently opening a conversation in the desert of Egypt were: "Abba, speak a word; how are we to be saved" or "Pray for me."[12] The same approach is transferred to Gaza in Palestine, as witnessed in the same *Letter* 55 quoted above and addressed to Barsanuphius by a fellow Copt monk:

> A certain elderly Egyptian man . . . addressed a letter . . . to the Great Old Man (for he, too, was Egyptian) requesting prayer and counsel for the benefit of his soul.

Response by Barsanuphius

> As for what you write to me . . . , namely "Pray for my sins," I also say the same to you, pray for my sins.

THE ASCETIC TEACHING OF THE LETTERS

It may sometimes be tempting to separate *abstract theology* from *ascetic practice*, categorizing under the first heading the theory of the monastic life as expressed by representatives of the more intellectual or contemplative currents, and under the second heading its application as experienced by the saintly yet unscholarly representatives of the more affective or simplistic ways. In this case, Barsanuphius and John would be relegated to the more "practical" and less "theological" representatives of the monastic tradition. Their correspondence, after all, makes only few references to doctrinal issues or to mystical visions.

[12]See, for instance, *Sayings*, Antony 16 and 19.

Nonetheless, it is not clear whether Barsanuphius and John would themselves be very comfortable with any such distinction between theology and asceticism. For them, work is not to be distinguished from prayer; nor is it a distraction from prayer (*Letter* 150). While their correspondence certainly offers balanced and practical advice about the spiritual life, it nevertheless also contains remarkable nuances and profound theological insights. For instance, *Letters* 600–607 deal with doctrinal questions—in relation to Origen of Alexandria, Evagrius of Pontus, and Didymus the Blind—posed by one of the monks in the community. If, however, the elders respond to such questions, it is true to claim that they do so primarily in deference to the queries of their disciples.

> God does not demand these things [i.e., questioning doctrinal matters] from us. Rather, God demands sanctification, purification, silence, and humility. Nevertheless, since I do not want to leave your thoughts unanswered, and I have been afflicted in my prayers to God in order that he might assure me in regard to this matter, I have been constrained by this dilemma, but chose rather to assume affliction for myself in order to relieve you of your own affliction. . . .

> For, you will not be asked about these matters on that day, as to why you do not understand them or why you have not learned about them. (*Letter* 604)[13]

Furthermore, although in most of their responses, Barsanuphius and John in fact deal with the toilsome journey of the ascetic struggle itself, they do also make certain references to the mystical goal of the spiritual life and to the delight of arriving there.

[13]Doctrinal and other ecclesiastical issues are also treated in certain other sections of the correspondence: for example, one will discover references to general issues (*Letter* 370), the Trinity (*Letters* 169 and 600), the Council of Nicaea (*Letters* 58 and 701), martyrdom (*Letter* 433), the Canons of the Church (*Letter* 170), the teaching of St John Chrysostom (*Letter* 464), deification (*Letter* 199), and relationships of bishops *vis à vis* heretics (*Letters* 694–702, 733–735, 775 and 792).

Having arrived at this point, they [the saints] attained to that measure where there is no agitation or distraction, becoming all intellect, all eye, all life, all light, all perfect, all gods.

They toiled, they were magnified, they were glorified, they shined, they were perfected. They lived, because first they died. They rejoice, and they make others also rejoice. (*Letter* 207)

Another distinction sometimes drawn is that between *the monastic life* and *the secular life*. Under the former heading are included all of the particular and austere practices identified with renouncing the world, such as assuming the Cross of Christ, and following him in total obedience, even to the point of death; and under the latter heading all of the more general and broader virtues to be acquired and vices to be avoided. The correspondence itself, however, makes it abundantly clear that Barsanuphius and John would not espouse such a distinction between the way of the desert and the way of the world. While most of their correspondence is addressed to a monastic audience, a significant portion is comprised of responses to lay persons asking similar questions and receiving similar responses about the spiritual life.

It must also be remembered, to adopt the words of Basil of Caesarea, that the ascetic life is none other than "the way according to Gospel."[14] In the spiritual life, there is no sharp demarcation between monastics and non-monastics; the monastic life is simply the Christian life, lived out in a particular way. The circumstances of the response may vary externally, but the path is essentially one. Monks are Christians who have discovered special possibilities of imitating Christ. And those married or in the world face—not so much particular impediments, but—the same invitation to approach God.

Each person is called to do that which one is doing, to be what one is supposed to be, to "follow one's ways" (*Letter* 840). The

[14]Cf. Basil, *Letter* 207.2, PG 32.761.

condition, of course, is that everyone must first "examine one's ways," variously described as "study," "attention," and "search." Indeed, on two occasions in one letter (no. 838), this arduous process is described as "groping in the darkness of one's heart."

Most of what the two Old Men have to state aims at awakening their listeners from despondency and lifting them from despair. In one striking phrase, the Other Old Man remarks: "Awaken the Jesus that lies asleep within" (*Letter* 182). They advise their disciples never to be overwhelmed by, but always to welcome the opportunity of temptations (*Letter* 496). They offer strength and support; this is what they do best, and this is also what they advise others to do (*Letter* 315). These elders are always positive: "Listen, child, for every passion there is a medicine; and for every sin there is proper repentance" (*Letter* 226). They identify with the joys and the sorrows of their spiritual children: "If I could fill these letters with tears and send them to you, since you have afflicted yourself; it would have been of greater benefit to you" (*Letter* 229).

Throughout the correspondence, they constantly stress the need for vigilance and violence in the ascetic struggle, the importance of discernment and humility in the spiritual life, and the place of gratitude and gladness in daily activity. An eloquent summary of their teaching is found in *Letter* 267:

> Labor to receive these [gifts] with toil of heart, and God will grant them to you continually; I am referring to warmth and prayer. For forgetfulness makes these vanish, while this forgetfulness is caused by negligence. As for the protection of your senses, every gift is granted with toil of heart. The gift of vigilance does not allow the thoughts to enter; but if they do enter, it does not allow them to cause any damage.
>
> May God grant you to be vigilant and alert. For the words "give thanks in all things" (1 Thess 5.18) constitute a command, especially in the matter that you indicated to me.

Finally, searching your faults in order to seek forgiveness is also very beneficial.

What follows is a brief overview—comprehensive, although by no means exhaustive—of twelve fundamental principles of the ascetic teaching of Barsanuphius and John, as gleaned from the correspondence of these two extraordinary elders.

1. *Continual vigilance*

The Gaza elders underline constant vigilance and alertness in every aspect of one's life. This criterion is fundamental in spiritual progress as well as daily practice:

> Pay attention then to yourself with vigilance, that you may set God before you at all times, so that the words of the prophet will be fulfilled: "I foresaw the Lord before my face continually, for the Lord is on my right hand so that I may not be moved" (Ps 15.8).

> Stretch out your hands with all your soul to the things that lie before you, and meditate on this continually, that you may hear the voice of God saying to you: "Behold, I am sending my angel before your face, to prepare your way before you" (Mt 11.10). (*Letter 7*)

Vigilance is a critical part of spiritual alertness and awareness. We are always called to "make a new beginning," say Barsanuphius and John.[15] It is, however, a beginning forged in light of an end. The reason for one's vigilance is the certainty of one's impending death, which becomes the focus for a more attentive life.

---

[15]The phrase "make a new beginning" is a copticism henceforth established in ascetic terminology. See *Letters* 55, 257, 266, 276, 493, 497, 500, 562, 614, and 788. Cf. also *Sayings*, Arsenius 3.

Be vigilant, brother, for you are mortal and ephemeral. Do not consent to lose eternal life for a fleeting moment. (*Letter* 256)

Pay attention to yourself, and expect your impending death. Say to yourself the words of the blessed Arsenius: "Arsenius, why did you leave the world?"[16] (ibid.)

2. *"Violence in all things"*

In light of this end, the struggle against the passions is ongoing. Nevertheless, it is also positive. Barsanuphius will often reply with the proverbial statement: "The untempted is also untested" (*Letter* 248). However, the reality is that this struggle to remain focused through attentiveness is not natural in a world of distraction and dissipation. This reality is highlighted with the concept of "violence," whereby "the kingdom of heaven is taken by force" (Mt 11.12).

Brother, "forcing oneself in all things" and humility brings one to progress. For even the Apostle says this: "We are afflicted in every way, but not crushed" (2 Cor 4.8). . . . This is why a person should not have one's own will but in everything blame oneself, and then that person shall find the mercy of God.

However, if the devil fools one into proudly thinking that one has done well, then everything that has been achieved is lost. Therefore, as you do whatever you do, humbly say: "Lord, forgive me, for I have burdened the Abbot, by casting on him my burden." The Lord Jesus Christ will save you. Amen. (*Letter* 243)

The monk unceasingly struggles against the "eight passions" (*Letter* 44), or—elsewhere—the "seven nations" (*Letter* 209), in order to

[16]See *Sayings*, Arsenius 40.

purify the "five senses" (*Letters* 208 and 612). The correspondence constantly emphasizes the fact that "you shall know them by their works" (Mt 7.16) or fruits (cf. *Letters* 22, 23, 94, 238, 401, 405, 453, 455).

3. *The gift of discernment*

Barsanuphius and John constantly underline the importance of balance and discretion. For instance, a monk who is ill should not also expect to fast because the body is already being strained and restrained by the illness itself (*Letter* 79; see also *Letter* 212). In all things and to all people, Barsanuphius and John recommend the middle, or royal, way in ascetic rigor. Such is the essence of discernment: "This is the way of the fathers: neither to be wasteful nor to be crushed in one's discipline" (*Letter* 212). For Barsanuphius, the virtue of discernment involves a profound awareness of one's attitude or "intention"[17] as well as the clear understanding of one's motivation or "disposition."[18] The two Old Men move beyond a rigid code of ethical prescriptions, with their almost inhumane consequences, into a more compassionate situational or occasional ethics, where there are no established formulas and fewer binding directives, where the individual always assumes responsibility for his or her actions.

Not only do people differ from one another (*Letter* 157); indeed, even circumstances within one and the same person may differ from time to time (*Letter* 842). This is why "conscience" plays an important role in these letters.[19] Conscience implies the integral knowledge of many aspects and factors that are interconnected and interdependent. It is a knowledge that is more intuitive than analytical, a knowledge that invites and involves the subconscious, the conscious and the supraconscious levels.

[17]See *Letters* 1, 60, (esp.) 239, 453, (also) 455, 472, 493, 611, 613, 648, and 720.
[18]See *Letters* (esp.) 17, 70, 462, and 646.
[19]See *Letters* 3, 13, (esp.) 275, 276, 462, 464, 633, 700, and 712.

4. The way of humility

> *Question* (no. 100) to the Great Old Man: Tell me, father,
> what does humility mean? Moreover, pray that the end of my
> life may be peaceful.

> *Response by Barsanuphius*

> Humility means regarding oneself as "earth and ashes" (Gen
> 18.27) in deeds and not just in words, and saying: "Who am
> I?" (2 Sam 7.18). "Who counts me as anything?" "I have noth-
> ing to do with anyone."

Humility is a self-emptying that resembles death. In order to learn
something new, one needs first to be emptied. Transformation
involves dying, although it is always seen in the context of resurrection. Learning becomes living. Humble endurance is also connected
to deep calmness (*Letter* 21).

5. Gratitude in all circumstances

Barsanuphius is quite clear on the priority and necessity of gratitude. Thanksgiving forms a central part of his teaching and is
reflected in numerous letters. "The words 'give thanks in all circumstances' (1 Thess 5.18) constitute an order" (*Letter* 267); "Let us never
lose our thanksgiving" (*Letter* 366). We are called to offer thanks to
God in all circumstances (*Letters* 2, 6, 29, 45, 191, 201, 351, 384, 574,
and 682), including adverse situations such as illness (*Letters* 174, 182,
197, 211, and 515). Such an act of gratitude comprises an act of true
sacrifice, which even itself constitutes an intercession on our behalf
before God. "In all things give thanks to God. For thanksgiving intercedes to God for our weakness!" (*Letter* 214).

6. Heavenly joy

Barsanuphius exclaims throughout his responses: "Rejoice in the Lord; rejoice in the Lord; rejoice in the Lord" (*Letters* 10 and 87). The joy that he is invoking upon his listeners and recipients is a divine joy; while it reaches below, it comes from above:

> May the God of our fathers bring you into this joy. For it contains ineffable light, and it is brilliant and sweet.

> It does not remember earthly nourishment, but seeks only what is above and mediates only what is above, where Christ is seated at the right hand of the Father. To him be the glory to the ages. Amen. (*Letter* 98, found only in the Athens ms.)

Yet, it is a state to which everyone may aspire. "May one rejoice in the Lord when one has reached the goal, and when one is about to reach it, and when one is still waiting to reach it" (*Letter* 137). One must struggle "to reach" this goal. Therefore, other fundamental principles of the ascetic way, according to Barsanuphius' and John's understanding of the tradition received from their own elders, include continual labor or "toil," total "obedience" and "submission," and the concepts—at once difficult to translate and difficult to apply—of acquiring the virtue of not reckoning oneself as anything (*to apsepheston*) and of avoiding the pretense to rights (*to dikaioma*).

7. Labor for love

Barsanuphius and John recognize that the entire ascetic effort of the monk is the result of synergy. In this way, the two elders reconcile the age-old dilemma of the ascetic Christian—in regard to the interplay between grace and nature (*Letter* 763).

Labor, however, is not merely laborious; the Greek term that is often adopted by Barsanuphius is "work" or "toil" (*ergon*), which also implies a sense of creativity. Certainly, the struggle is difficult, because every monk will resist change, pain, passion, and death. Yet, the result is again positive; it is a labor *of* love and a labor *for* love. This is evident throughout the correspondence:

> Therefore, labor, brother, so that you may find even more love and rest. For before the boat reaches the harbor, it is beaten and tossed by the waves and the storms. However, once it reaches the harbor, it then finds itself in a state of great calm. (*Letter* 9)

> Brother, no one can be saved from the passions or please God without labor of heart and contrition. (*Letter* 256)

> Pay attention to yourself, brother; for it is impossible to be saved without labor and humility. (*Letter* 240)

The clearest evidence that one is laboring for love lies in the fulfillment of the Apostolic commandment to "bear one another's burdens" (Gal 6.2), which is nothing less than an imitation of the example set by Christ (cf. Mt 11.28–30). This Pauline text is quoted in numerous *Letters*,[20] while the Old Men themselves explicitly bear the burdens of their own disciples—sometimes only half the burden,[21] at other times two-thirds of the burden,[22] while on other occasions even the entire burden![23]

> I admire your love, brother, but you do not understand the affairs of love that is according to God. . . . Yet, if I say something to someone beyond my measure, or beyond my power, I speak moved by the love of Christ, knowing—as I said— that I am nothing but a worthless slave. Since then you did

[20]See, for instance, *Letters* 94, 96, 104, 108, 123, 239, 243, 483, 575a, 579, and 604.
[21]See *Letters* 70 and 72.
[22]See *Letter* 73.
[23]See *Letters* 73, 553, and 833.

not understand what I told you, namely that I bear half your sins, I have made you a partner with me. For I did not say to you: "I bear one-third," leaving you to bear more and be burdened more than I. And again, I said what I have said in order to banish self-love; this is why I did not speak to you of bearing two-thirds, showing myself to be stronger than you; for such conduct would be vainglory. And I did not say: "I bear the whole." This belongs to the perfect, to those who have become brothers of Christ, who laid down his own life for our sake, and who loved those who have loved us with perfect love in order to do this. . . . However, if you wish to cast on me the whole burden, then for the sake of obedience I accept this too. Forgive me that great love leads me to talking nonsense. (*Letter* 73)

8. Obedience and spiritual direction

Obedience is the glue that binds elder and disciple; yet, above and beyond this, it is also the way in which the entire community is held together. "Therefore, doing everything on the order of the Abbot and not according to one's own will is the sign of communality and equality with the brothers in the monastery" (*Letter* 250). The ascetic struggle is clearly arduous, but the spiritual journey is not supposed to be undertaken alone. Obedience, humility, submission, guidance, seeking counsel, and cutting off one's own will are all part and parcel of the spiritual way.

Obedience cuts off the will, but without toil no one can acquire obedience. If you are sitting here for the sake of obedience and not for bodily comfort, then this is not the result of your own will; nor again are you sitting passionately but rather you are pleasing God. If, however, you are sitting here in order to receive pleasure from comfort, then you are not pleasing God. (*Letter* 249)

Obedience is perhaps one of the most critical elements of the ascetic way, a crucial aspect of taking up one's cross, and an indispensable characteristic of the genuine monastic. Quite simply put, "a monk should not hold onto his own will *at all in anything*" (*Letter* 288, my emphasis).

In this respect, perhaps one of the most striking elements of the Old Men's teaching is their conviction that, as spiritual guides of their disciples, they dare also to assume responsibility for them before God.

> *Question* (no. 270). Request from the same brother to the same Great Old Man, that he might bear his sins.
>
> *Response*
>
> Brother, although you are asking of me something that is beyond me, nevertheless I shall show you the limits of love, namely that it forces itself to move even beyond its own limits. Behold, I have admired you as a person, and I assume responsibility for you and bear you. Nevertheless, I do so on this condition, that you also bear the keeping of my words and commandments; for they bring you salvation. In this way, you shall live without reproach.

Barsanuphius and John are constantly careful not to interfere in or impose themselves upon the spiritual development of their correspondents:

> Simple advice according to God is one thing, and a command is another. A command has an inviolable bond; but advice is counsel without compulsion, showing a person the straight way in life. (*Letter* 368)

Indeed, it would be more appropriate in their case to say that the spiritual director is spiritually *identified with* rather than externally *authoritative over* the spiritual disciple: "The Lord has bound your soul to mine, saying: 'Do not leave him.' Therefore, it is not for me to teach you, but in fact to learn from you" (*Letter* 164).

9. *Not reckoning oneself as anything* (or *to apsepheston*)

This virtue is both difficult to acquire and difficult to apply. Barsanuphius frequently offers the following kind of advice to those who approach him:

> Be carefree from all things; then, you will have time for God. Die to all people; for, this is true exile. Moreover, retain the virtue of not reckoning yourself as anything; then, you will find your thought to be undisturbed. In addition, do not consider yourself as having done anything good; thus, your reward will be kept whole. (*Letter* 259)

> Therefore, you should keep your tongue from idle talk, your stomach from pleasure, refrain from irritating your neighbor, stay modest, do not reckon yourself as anything, love everyone, and always have God in your intellect, remembering the time when you will appear before God's countenance. Keep these things, and your soil will yield an hundredfold (cf. Mt 4.8) in fruits for God, to whom be the glory to the ages. Amen. (*Letter* 271)

Barsanuphius is specifically asked to explain this complicated notion, which is so central to his teaching.

> *Question* (no. 227) to the Great Old Man: Father, what does it mean not to reckon oneself as anything?[24]

---

[24]Dorotheus of Gaza develops this theme of his master in his *Spiritual Works*, *Letter* 2.

Response

Brother, not reckoning oneself as anything means not equating oneself with anyone and not saying anything in regard to any good deed that you may also have achieved.

Barsanuphius knows that he is not in any way innovating in this aspect of his teaching, which he attributes to the Desert Fathers of Egypt (*Letter* 604). However, the concept does assume greater significance in his teaching.

10. *The pretense to rights* (or *to dikaioma*)

Once again, the Great Old Man is asked to explain what this complex virtue implies and to describe its origin. In his responses, he embraces the notions of self-justification, self-trust and self-deceit.

What is the pretense to rights?

Response

The pretense to rights is something that does not contain arrogance, but rather contains the denial of fault, in the manner of Adam and Eve and Cain and others who sinned, but who later denied their sin in order to justify themselves. (*Letter* 477)

Such is the origin of this concept, which nevertheless contains several dimensions that are revealed or discerned in various ways in the spiritual life.

The desire that comes from the demons is what we call pretense to rights and trust in oneself. Through these, one is entirely taken captive. (*Letter* 173)

> Nothing that occurs with turmoil is good, but always from the power of the devil through our pretense to rights. (*Letter* 724)

Clearly, Barsanuphius is here drawing on his long experience and spiritual appropriation of the desert tradition, where the monk was never evasively to blame other people or situations but always directly to assume the burden of personal responsibility.

> Abba Antony said to Abba Poemen: "This is the great work of a person: always to take the blame for one's own sins before God and to expect temptation to the last breath."[25]

Finally, if we were to consider the goal itself of the ascetic life in the teaching of Barsanuphius and John, then the magnitude of the correspondence might be condensed into two principal virtues, namely *prayer* (indeed, unceasing prayer) and *tears* (in fact, continual tears).

11. Learning to pray

Prayer is the activity of the monk at all times and in all places.

> *Question* (no. 441). When I am sitting down, either reading or doing my handiwork, and want to pray, I am not sure whether I should be sitting. The same happens even if I have my head covered. Moreover, when I am walking about and want to pray, my thought demands that I turn toward the east. What should I do, father?

> *Response*

> Whether you are sitting down or walking about, whether you are working or eating, or whatever else you are doing—

[25]Cf. Antony, *Saying* 4.

even if you are performing your bodily need—whether you happen to be turned toward the east or toward the west, do not hesitate to pray.

For we have been commanded to pray without ceasing (cf. 1 Thess 5.17) and to do so in every place (cf. 1 Tim 2.8). Again, it has been written: "Prepare the way for the one who rides toward the west; his name is the Lord" (Ps 67.5), which shows that God is everywhere. Moreover, when you have your head covered, do not cease praying. Simply make sure that you are not doing this in contempt.

The elders offer specific and detailed advice about how to pray without ceasing, especially in difficult situations, as well as how to respond when it appears that one's prayers are of no benefit (see *Letters* 182 and 710–711).

12. Learning to weep

We know that the Other Old Man, John, never took Holy Communion without shedding tears (*Letter* 570), something echoing the earlier Desert Fathers, such as Arsenius of Scetis in the preceding century, but also foreshadowing later monastic writers, such as John Climacus and Abba Isaac the Syrian in the following century, and Symeon the New Theologian as late as the tenth century.

This emphasis on tears is equally shared by both of the elders of Gaza. Indeed, Barsanuphius is quick to distinguish the phenomenon of tears from any negative expression of guilt that looks backward, describing it rather as a positive expression of longing and desire for a grace that was lost, but which yet lies ahead. "One who is conscious of what has been lost will weep for it. Moreover, one who sincerely desires something will endure many travels and afflictions, in the hope of achieving that, which is desired" (*Letter* 400).

John the Prophet is asked to provide a synthesis for the teachings about the inner and outer dispositions of joy and sorrow alike, a combination that will forever be consolidated in ascetic literature through the teaching of John Climacus (c. 579–c. 659), who will later be inspired to write in a unique fashion about "joyful sorrow" in step seven of his *Ladder of Divine Ascent.*

> *Question* (no. 730). Since the Lord said: "Blessed are they that mourn" (Mt 5.4) and the Apostle says: "Be joyful and cheerful" (Rom 12.8), what should one do in order to appear to be both mournful and cheerful? In addition, how can both of these, mournfulness and cheerfulness, exist in one and the same person?
>
> *Response*
>
> Mourning is sorrow according to God, which gives rise to repentance. The characteristics of repentance are fasting, psalmody, prayer, and meditation on the words of God. Cheerfulness is gladness according to God, which is revealed through modesty in word and conduct when people encounter one another. Therefore, let your heart have mourning, while your conduct and words should have modest gladness; then, both virtues may coexist.

MONASTICISM AND SACRAMENTS

Many of the early monastic texts are curiously silent about the sacramental life of the hermits and communities. For instance, in his *Life of Antony*, Athanasius, the Archbishop of Alexandria, makes no explicit reference to the question as to whether the Father of the Monks received Holy Communion while in his outer or inner desert. Evagrius of Pontus makes little if any reference to the sacraments in his formative and influential treatises. And in his undisputable masterpiece of monastic literature, *The Ladder of Divine*

Ascent, John Climacus makes no explicit mention at all of the sacrament of Holy Communion, although he does refer to the sacrament of Baptism in his chapter on tears.

Such a reticence about the sacraments neither constitutes the established rule nor implies that these authors undermine the significance or centrality of sacraments in the spiritual and even in the ascetic life. Indeed, even as prominent a Pope of Rome as Gregory the Great does not refer to the sacrament of the Eucharist in his famous *Moralia*. Perhaps certain representatives of monastic literature take the sacraments for granted; or perhaps they do not consider it a part of their task at hand to include them in their writing. Whatever the case may be, there are clearly certain significant exceptions to this "rule" of silence in regard to sacraments among monastic authors. For instance, in the early fifth century, Mark the Monk assumes the sacrament of baptism as the central principle for his teaching. And in the sixth century, Barsanuphius and John undoubtedly stand out as notable exceptions and advocates of the sacramental life.

Several letters refer to the importance of baptism into the faith of the Nicaean Fathers (*Letters* 58 and 694), to salvation that derives from baptism as deliverance from death to life (*Letters* 62 and 211), to the baptism of heretics (*Letters* 820–822). Other letters refer to the forgiveness of sins through the prayer (Jas 5.16) and power (Jn 20.23) of the saints, who are able to bind and loose (*Letters* 10, 107, 194, 220, 226, 233, 240, 277, 345, 359, 399, 404, 444, and 543), but also through the sacrament of unction (Jas 5.14–15; cf. also *Letter* 211).

Beyond this, however, there are other letters that refer to liturgical customs and gestures (*Letters* 4, 241, and 742), to liturgical cycles and offices (*Letters* 32, 50, 143, 169, 178, 209, 334, 427–428, 519, 739, 751, and 821), as well as to the specific act of participating in the sacred mystery of Holy Communion (*Letters* 241, 334, 404, and 463–464), which Barsanuphius describes as: "Incorruptible sacrifice, offered for the life of the world. The one who truly eats thereof is also sacrificed and not dominated by spiritual corruption" (*Letter* 137b).

The monk is to approach with fear of God, faith, and love (*Letters* 170, 241, and 244), with humility and without vainglory (*Letters* 742 and 821), in order to participate without condemnation (*Letters* 170 and 570b). Indeed, if the monk is unwell, he may even partake of the sacred mysteries in his own cell (*Letter* 212).

STRUGGLE AND STAGES IN THE DEVELOPMENT OF SPIRITUAL WISDOM

The *Letters* of Barsanuphius and John, and especially those addressed by and to Dorotheus of Gaza (*Letters* 252–338), present another significant development.[26] They reveal an element that gradually disappears from the ascetic literature, and especially from the *Sayings of the Desert Fathers*, even as these begin to be collated and edited. For, the original or oral transmission of the wisdom of the Egyptian desert preserved the spontaneity of the profound advice and impressive actions of the Desert Fathers and Mothers.

However, during the stage of their transition from an oral culture to a written text, the *Sayings* inevitably and distinctively became a little more static. As a result, readers begin to lose sight of the personal element that originally sparked these living and life-giving words. More especially, later readers misplace the process and struggle that initially shaped these personal and fiery words. Therefore, what is "received" is the intense drop of wisdom, however without the consecutive stages that led to the final product. What is missing is the ongoing process and grueling struggle—all of the contentions, hesitations and limitations of the spiritual aspirant. The *Sayings of the Desert Fathers*, for instance, often present the spiritual reality in *the way that it should be*, rather than in *the way that it is*—with all the denials, the doubts, and the temptations.

---

[26]There are ninety-three letters addressed to Dorotheus of Gaza, seventy-two of these from John and twenty-one of them from Barsanuphius.

Yet, in Barsanuphius and John, we are allowed to witness each of the painful stages unfolding in graduating and slow motion. Their *correspondence* provides a personal and cultural context for the earlier *apophthegmata*. What might normally have taken place on the level of a face-to-face encounter is here recorded in writing, with all of the mutuality or back-and-forth of a personal relationship. Neither the authors of the letters nor the compiler of the correspondence seek to conceal the innate challenges and tensions of the spiritual process itself. As the French translator of this correspondence, Fr Lucien Regnault, has eloquently written: "What the *Sayings of the Desert Fathers* allow us to glimpse only in the form of fleeting images, is here played out like a film before our very eyes."[27]

The following exchange of letters is one of several examples that highlight this progressive development and struggle to understand the subtleties and insights of the spiritual way in an exchange between elder and disciple that betrays also the involvement of divine grace:

> *Question* (no. 293) from the same brother to the same Old Man: If a brother does something insignificant, yet I am afflicted by this act on account of my own will, what should I do? Should I keep silent and not give rest to my heart, or should I speak to him with love and not remain troubled? Moreover, if the matter afflicts others, and not me, should I speak for the sake of the others? Or would this appear as if I have just taken on a cause?

> *Response by John*

> If it is a matter that is not sinful but insignificant, and you speak simply in order to give rest to your heart, then it is to your defeat. For you were not able to endure it as a result of your weakness.

[27] Cf. *Barsanuphe et Jean de Gaza: Correspondance* (Abbaye de Solesmes: 1972), 6.

Just blame yourself and be silent. However, if the matter afflicts others, tell your Abbot; and whether he speaks or else tells you to speak, you will be carefree.

Question (no. 294) from the same person to the same Old Man: If I speak to the Abbot for the sake of the others, I suspect that the brother will be troubled; so what should I do? And if he afflicts both the others and me, should I speak for the sake of the others, or should I keep silent in order not to satisfy myself? If I suspect that he will not be grieved, should I also speak for myself, or should I force myself against this?

Response by John

As far as the turmoil of the brother is concerned, if you speak to the Abbot, then you have nothing to worry about. When it is necessary to speak for the sake of others, and you are worried about it, then speak for them. As for yourself, always force yourself not to speak.

Question (no. 295). Question from the same brother to the same Old Man: But my thought tells me that if my brother is troubled against me, he will become my enemy, thinking that I slandered him to the Abbot.

Response by John

This thought of yours is wicked; for it wants to prevent you from correcting your brother. Therefore, do not prevent yourself from speaking; but rather, speak according to God.

For, indeed, even sick people that are being healed will speak against their doctors; yet, the latter do not care, knowing that the same people will thank them afterward.

Question (no. 296) from the same person to the same Old Man: If I examine my thought and notice that it is not for the sake of my brother's benefit that I wish to speak to the Abbot, but with the purpose of slandering him, should I speak or keep silent?

Response by John

Advise your thought to speak according to God and not for the sake of slander. And if your thought is conquered by criticism, even so, speak to your Abbot and confess to him your criticism, so that both of you may be healed—the one who was at fault and the one who was critical.

Question (no. 297) from the same to the same: If my thought does not allow me to confess to the Abbot that I am speaking to him with the purpose of slandering the brother, what should I do? Should I speak or not?

Response

Do not say anything to him, and the Lord will take care of the matter. For it is not necessary for you to speak when this harms your soul. God will take care of the brother's correction as God pleases.

The same graduation of argument and maturation of thought is discerned in other letters on matters relating to prayer (*Letters* 427–431 and 438–447), good deeds (*Letters* 401–413 and 679–680), habits (*Letters* 433–437), legal issues (*Letters* 650–651, 667–673, 687, 720–721, 725–726), spiritual thoughts (*Letters* 448–449), the treatment of servants (653–657), conversations with friends (*Letters* 469–476 and 707–709), blessing a meal (*Letters* 716–719), dealing with real estate (*Letters* 486–488 and 648), problems in personal relationships (*Letters* 489–491 and 662), doctrinal issues (*Letters* 602–607 and

694–704), and almsgiving (*Letters* 617–636). These series reveal the intimate connection between the desert tradition of Egypt and the epistolary tradition of Gaza.[28]

The Formation and Legacy of Barsanuphius and John

Barsanuphius and John certainly seem to display characteristics both *in common with* as well as *in contrast to* their predecessors, the desert dwellers of Egypt. For instance, each of the prominent elders of Gaza is balanced and unpolemical in their nature and in their counsel, much like the disposition of the Egyptian monastics, whose sayings are preserved in their collections. The correspondence of Barsanuphius and John does not in general reveal the confessional rifts that affected so much of Christendom during this period, preferring to remain deliberately reticent on the divisive and complex doctrinal debates of the sixth century.

The Old Men are far less militant and far more moderate than other representatives of both the Chalcedonian and non-Chalcedonian circles. Nowhere, for example, in the vast epistolary collection of Barsanuphius and John is there any clear or explicit condemnation or defense of the Chalcedonian definition. Their disciples were advised to abstain from such debates as well as from condemning those who chose to take sides. Other contemporary ascetics, such as Sabas (d. 532), while compassionate and non-judgmental in their outlook, are nevertheless deliberately and defensively concerned with confessional doctrine. Earlier, Peter the Iberian (c. 409–c. 488) is actively involved in the Christological controversy and

---

[28]In the present selection, I have maintained a capital letter for "Fathers" or "Elders," where this refers to the spiritual or even literary tradition of the Egyptian monastics found in such texts as *The Sayings of the Desert Fathers*. The regional and textual influence and relationship between the Egyptian elders and their Gaza successors is developed below.

openly opposed to the Chalcedonian supporters. It is no wonder, then, that an icon of the Great Old Man graces the frescoes depicting altar-cloths in the Great Church of Holy Wisdom in Constantinople, beside those of Antony of Egypt and Ephraim the Syrian. This is perhaps why Theodore the Studite (759–826) was anxious to defend and affirm the orthodoxy of Barsanuphius, John, and Dorotheus, as well as of Isaiah of Scetis before them.[29]

Yet, at the same time, the Gaza elders differ from their Egyptian counterparts inasmuch as they are overall more educated and widely read. This feature may not be unknown among the Desert Fathers, but it is rather exceptional. In general, it appears to be a characteristic of Palestinian monasticism.[30] Monks in the community of Seridos were familiar with the writings of Origen of Alexandria, Didymus the Blind, and Evagrius of Pontus (*Letter* 600). Barsanuphius' responses to questions about Origenist tendencies among certain representatives of the monastic tradition, together with John's explanations of the Great Old Man's words (*Letters* 601–607), reveal two elders who appreciate fine intellectual distinctions and discussions without at the same time being absorbed by these to the detriment of their prayer life or spiritual relationships. Thus, in another set of thirteen questions (between *Letters* 151 and 167), comprising responses to a certain Euthymius whose mind is almost obsessed with allegorical interpretations and details, Barsanuphius will recommend humility and silence!

[29]Barsanuphius chose to adopt the rhetoric of the non-Chalcedonian party, while urging his disciples to follow a Chalcedonian bishop. See the *Testament* of Theodore the Studite in PG 88.1813–1816 and PG 99.1028. These three had been anathematized by Patriarch Sophronius of Jerusalem in a synodical letter to Patriarch Sergius of Constantinople in 634: cf. PG 87. iii: 3192–3193. The orthodoxy of Barsanuphius was in question because of his reference in *Letter* 701 only to the First Ecumenical Council in Nicaea (325), without however making any mention of the Fourth Ecumenical Council in Chalcedon (451). The iconographic tradition, however, is also particularly interesting in light of the fact that the two Old Men permitted so few people to meet them in person.

[30]In the *Life of Cyriacus* (ch. 14) and the *Life of Sabas* (ch. 83), Cyril of Scythopolis refers to the monks of Palestine as "more lettered" than others. Cf. transl. R. Price, *Lives of the Monks of Palestine* (Kalamazoo, MI: Cistercian Publications, 1990).

The Old Men Barsanuphius and John, and particularly their gifted disciple Dorotheus of Gaza, sense that they are a *part of a new tradition*, closely linked to the past and yet at the same time clearly looking to a different age and a different environment. Barsanuphius and John are forward-looking to the diverse monastic population that they serve and the diverse monastic culture that they confront. They are conscious of the need for greater tolerance and openness in communal (monastic) and social (secular) relations. In fact, the presence of these two elders in the region of Gaza, that intersection and cross-section of so many peoples and pilgrims, brought together so many pieces from the worlds of Egypt, Sinai, Palestine, Asia Minor, Syria, and as far east as Persia. The same region also numbered Arabs, Greeks, Latins, Armenians, Georgians, and others.

It is no wonder that the monks of this region were deeply influenced by Barsanuphius' openness toward foreigners imposed by a dynamic of positive interaction.[31] Indeed, Barsanuphius was quite clear about the role of his contemporaries; it was, as he determines in *Letter* 569, to pray for the salvation of the whole world, both Orthodox and non-Orthodox, pious and pagan alike:

> There are three men, perfect in God, who have exceeded the measure of humanity and received the authority to loose and bind, to forgive and hold sins. These three stand before the shattered world, keeping the whole world from complete and sudden annihilation.

> Through their prayers, God combines his chastisement with his mercy. Moreover, it has been told to them, that God's wrath will last a little longer. . . .

> These three are John in Rome and Elias in Corinth, and another in the region of Jerusalem. I believe that they will

[31] See *Letters* 686, 733 and 777. Cf. also I.A. Voulgarakis, "Missionsangaben in den Briefen der Asketen Barsanuphius und Johannes," in A. Kallis, ed., *Philoxenia* (Munster, 1980).

achieve God's great mercy. Yes, they will undoubtedly
achieve it. Amen.

It is quite possible that Barsanuphius possessed the discerning boldness and humble conviction before God and humanity to claim
within his heart that he was the third of these ascetics.[32]

THE *LETTERS* THROUGH THE TRADITION:
SOURCES AND INFLUENCES

In spite of the fact that there are almost no proper names contained
in the *Letters* themselves, the sources with which Barsanuphius and
John are clearly familiar include the *Sayings of the Desert Fathers* of
Egypt (and especially Evagrius of Pontus), *The Lives of the Fathers*
(and especially that of Pachomius), as well as earlier monastic
fathers and writers, such as Basil the Great and Isaiah of Scetis. In
this respect, the basic insights of the correspondence are drawn from
the spirituality of the early Egyptian desert. They are essentially letters from the desert. They comprise more than mere anecdotes in
the light of and in the likeness of the *Sayings of the Desert Fathers*.
They present profound analyses of the fundamental concepts of that
lifestyle and spirituality.

The *Sayings of the Desert Fathers*, in both their alphabetical and
anonymous or systematic collections, are already found in seminal
texts of the time. Such texts include the *Praktikos* as well as the *Chap-
ters on Prayer* by Evagrius (d. 399); the *Institutes* of John Cassian (d.c.
430); the *Life of Saint Melanie the Younger* (d. 439), attributed to her
confidant and chaplain Gerontius and dating to the middle of the
fifth century; the *Ascetic Discourses* of Isaiah of Scetis (d.c. 489); the
Life of Saint Euthymius (d. 473), written by Cyril of Scythopolis in
the latter half of the sixth century; and the *Reflections* of Zosimas

---

[32]This is the estimation of Nikodemus of Mount Athos in his foreword to the
Volos edition of the *Letters* of Barsanuphius and John, published by S. Schoinas.

(d.c. 530), who founded a community in the first half of the sixth century.

Abba Isaiah of Scetis inserts numerous *Sayings*, both recognizable and original, in his *Ascetic Discourses*, possibly regarding himself as responsible for preserving and promoting the words of the elders with whom he was personally acquainted in Egypt.

In content and style, Zosimas' *Reflections* very much resemble the *Ascetic Discourses* of Abba Isaiah of Scetis. Zosimas' treatise makes numerous citations to the *Sayings*, implying perhaps that the latter may have borrowed these from existing written texts. Euthymius and Zosimas reveal having heard from others various sayings, which attests to the fact that these were widely known and, possibly, even accessible more or less everywhere in monastic circles of lower Palestine by the middle of the sixth century.

Indeed, Zosimas' reference to "the *Apophthegmata* of the Holy Elders" is perhaps the earliest such characterization of the *Sayings* with this specific title. Like the *Sayings of the Desert Fathers* themselves, the "reflections" were "spoken" and not written down by Zosimas. In fact, the *Reflections* indicate that: "The blessed Zosimas loved to read these *Sayings* all the time; they were almost like the air that he breathed. It is from these *Sayings* that he came to receive the fruit of every virtue."[33]

Zosimas flourished between 475 and 525, from the period just after the Fourth Ecumenical Council (451) until around the time of the great Gaza elders, Barsanuphius, John, and Dorotheus. He is mentioned several times by Dorotheus of Gaza, who knew him personally and visited him as his younger contemporary and compatriot. Dorotheus may in fact be the compiler of the *Reflections* themselves. Fr Lucien Regnault especially highlights the influential role of the monasteries of Seridos and of Dorotheus in the Gaza region, and the *Letters* of Barsanuphius and John as well as the *Works*

---

[33]Zosimas, *Reflections*, ch.12b (Avgoustinos edition, Jerusalem, 1913), 17. Translation and introduction by J. Chryssavgis, *In the Heart of the Desert: The Spirituality of the Desert Fathers and Mothers* (World Wisdom Publications, 2003). Also found in John Moschus, *Spiritual Meadow*, ch. 212 PG 87.3104–3105.

of their disciple Dorotheus, all of which offer the richest documentation in this regard.[34]

The *Letters* of Barsanuphius and John frequently quote or evoke the *Sayings*. There are at least eighty direct references to the *Apophthegmata* themselves, while numerous phrases recommend them as a basis for spiritual practice and progress, sometimes by name (sixteen times) but mostly by implication (thirty-four times). On other occasions, the Old Men adopt alternative phrases:

The fathers have said (fourteen times)
It is written in the fathers (once)
It is written in the elders (once)
It is written in the *Sayings of the Elders* (twice)
The *Lives of the Fathers* (twice)
The *Sayings of the Fathers* (once)
The *Sayings of the Fathers* and their *Lives* (twice)
The *Life of the Fathers* and the responses (once)
The books of the elders (once)
The *Gerontika* (once).

There are at least fifty-five direct references to the *Sayings of the Desert Fathers* in the writings of Dorotheus alone. He also seems to be the first writer to designate the *Apophthegmata* as *The Gerontikon* (or *The Book of the Old Men*).[35] Might, therefore, this Dorotheus also be one of those responsible for the collection of the *Sayings* themselves? Certainly, Dorotheus is the only ancient witness to the single saying attributed to Basil in the alphabetical collection of the *Sayings of the Desert Fathers*,[36] while both Barsanuphius and Dorotheus refer to the *Rules* of St Basil.

[34]L. Regnault, "Les *Apophtegmes des Pères* en Palestine aux Ve et VIe siècles," *Irénikon* 54 (1981): 320–30.

[35]See his *Teachings* I, 13 PG 88.1633C, and *Sources Chrétiennes* 92 (Paris: Cerf, 1952). G.W.H. Lampe's *Patristic Lexikon* (Oxford: Oxford University Press, 1991), 313, refers, for this word, to a letter by Nilus; however, this is not an authentic letter of Nilus.

[36]See L. Regnault, "Les *Apophtegmes* des Pères," 328; and Dorotheus, *Teachings* 24, in *Sources Chrétiennes* 92 (Paris: Cerf, 1952), 182–84.

The influence of the two Old Men, while limited owing to their moderate appeal to the Council of Chalcedon (451) and their conservative criticism of its opponents, is especially evident in their gifted and renowned disciple, Dorotheus of Gaza, and on the disciple of their disciple, Dositheus the Younger.[37] It is also apparent in later monastic authorities, such as John Climacus,[38] Theodore the Studite,[39] Symeon the New Theologian, and Kallistos/Ignatios Xanthopoulos.[40]

The surviving manuscripts attest to the fact that the correspondence of Barsanuphius and John was early appreciated and disseminated. Although the Moslem invasions of Palestine left little or nothing in that region to remind one of the monastic or Byzantine presence and influence,[41] yet the correspondence was certainly known in late eighth- and early ninth-century Constantinople, particularly in the work of Patriarch Tarasius and the writings of Theodore the Studite. The late tenth- and early eleventh-century anthology on prayer, the *Synagoge* of Paulos Evergetinos,[42] cites almost a third of the *Letters*, seventy from John and thirteen from Barsanuphius. The emphasis (some forty-seven *Letters*) is on the correspondence between the elders and Dorotheus of Gaza.

The oldest extant manuscripts originate on Mt Sinai and date from the tenth century. These are Georgian translations, but only contain around seventy-nine letters of the correspondence.[43] One of these is entitled: "Teachings of the Blessed Barsanuphius and John" (cf. Sinai 34), while the other (cf. Sinai 35) is dated 907 and entitled:

[37]See the edition of *The Life of Dositheus the Younger* in *Orientalia Christiana* 26.78 (Rome, 1932), 850–124.

[38]See especially *Step* 26 of the *Ladder of Divine Ascent*, in PG 88.1093.

[39]See his *Testament* in PG 99.1816.

[40]Indeed, the fourteenth-century Hesychasts appear to espouse Barsanuphius and John as their patrons in their doctrine on silence and prayer.

[41]J. Pargoire, *L' Eglise Byzantine de 527 à 847* (Paris, 1905), 274f.

[42]Published in Venice (1783) and reissued in Constantinople (1861) and Athens (fifth edition between 1957–1966).

[43]The 1971 tranlsation of the Abbaye Saint Pierre de Solesmes also includes the letters translated from the Georgian by B. Outtier.

"Questions and Responses."[44] Several manuscripts are preserved on Mt Athos from the eleventh century through the fourteenth century, but also in Paris, Oxford, Athens, Moscow, Munich, Jerusalem, and Patmos. Some manuscripts have only certain letters; others only contain fragments. While there are no manuscripts from the fifteenth to the seventeenth centuries, there are several manuscripts from the eighteenth century alone.

J. Grinaeus first published nine of the letters by John the Prophet in Basel, 1569, together with the works of Abba Dorotheus. In Paris, 1715, B. Montfaucon published the letters relating to Origenism. In volume 86 (columns 892–901) of the *Patrologia Graeca*, published in Paris during the mid- to late-nineteenth century, J.-P. Migne included *Letters* 600–604 of Barsanuphius and John, which deal with Origen, Evagrius, and Didymus, while volume 88 (columns 1812–1820) contains the letters of the correspondence addressed to Dorotheus of Gaza. From the late eighteenth century, several translations appeared in Moldavian, Slavonic,[45] and even in Russian, albeit sometimes partial to begin with, but complete by the end of the nineteenth century.

In the present translation, I have consulted both manuscript and contemporary sources, consulting the Bodleian Cromwell 18 (B) from Oxford as well as the Vatopedi 2 from Mt Athos. I have also relied on the text adopted by the most recent French edition, which is both critical and careful in its scholarship, being the result of a team of scholars over a number of years.[46]

Moreover, I have also considered the partial English edition and translation of Derwas Chitty[47] as well as those of the modern Greek

[44]Cf. G. Garitte, *Corpus Scriptorum Christianorum Orientalium* 165, Subsidia 9 (Louvain, 1956), 97 and 116–17. Also see E. Metreveli, *Collection sinaïtique de l' Institut des manuscripts* (Tiflis, 1978), 94 and 126–27.

[45]The Moldavian and early Slavonic translations were directed by Paissy Velichkovsky on the basis of an Athonite manuscript as early as 1794.

[46]See *Barsanuphe et Jean de Gaza: Correspondance*, volumes I-III, in *Sources Chrétiennes* 426–27, 450–51, and 468 (Paris, 1997–2002), critical text, notes, and index by F. Neyt and P. de Angelis-Noah.

[47]Rev. D. Chitty translated and published 124 letters in 1966, not long prior to his

publication by the Monastery of St John the Forerunner in Kareas, Athens.[48] Finally, I have referred to the edition by Nikodemus of Mount Athos, the first complete edition of Barsanuphius and John, based on several Athonite monasteries and originally published in Venice in 1816; this work was reprinted by S. Schoinas in Volos in 1960.[49]

Any translation will inevitably and almost naturally respond to the vibrant conversational style of these occasional and personal letters of the Old Men. This personal element is perhaps the most appealing to a contemporary reader. I have endeavored to remain as faithful to the original text as possible, however, without losing the spontaneous flavor of the letters themselves. For instance, where the Greek will sometimes simply say: "From the same to the same," I have elaborated depending on the context to say: "Letter from the same person (or brother) to the same Old Man."

The letters chosen for this selection are mostly from the briefer ones, which are of general interest to readers for purposes of information or inspiration. Therefore, I have not included longer letters or letters that presume deeper knowledge of monastic theology and spirituality or the historical context of the manuscript and its teaching. Altogether, there are—beyond the title and prologue of the work—one hundred and sixty-six letters that have been included. The selection embraces letters of advice from the elders to a variety of disciples—monks, clergy of all ranks (deacons, priests, and bishops), as well as laity—on a variety of subjects. I have also included a number of letters that are connected in the form of a series[50] on such topics as temptation and thoughts, as well as almsgiving and

death in 1971. Chitty compared Coislianus 124, Vatopedi 2, Nikodemus and Sinaiticus 411S for his critical edition. However, he has also prepared the translation of *Letters* 125–249. A copy of this text exists in the library of St Gregory's House in Oxford, England.

[48]Another Greek translation has been published in Thessalonika by Byzantion Editions in 1988–1989.

[49]Nikodemus' text contains certain repetitions as well as certain errors and *lacunas*, partly corrected by Schoinas. See bibliography below for details.

[50]See above, pp. 44–45.

conversation. The introduction includes numerous and large excerpts of letters not otherwise included in the selection itself in order to provide a clearer and fuller picture of the complete document.[51]

Inasmuch as this book comprises a selection, I have chosen to add the name of the responding elder, where this was missing or unclear in the text itself, in order for readers to know whether the response is from Barsanuphius or else from John. Nevertheless, I have also added notes denoting the provenance of the questions themselves—who is actually writing to the Old Men, including the occasions when it is laymen who are addressing the questions—since any selection inevitably conceals this point of clarification through omission. The same notes also explain whether the response is part of a series of letters addressed to a particular individual. This is important inasmuch as much of the correspondence and its content build upon and are completed in preceding or subsequent letters. Moreover, I have also created a brief title for each letter, often a summary of or else even an excerpt from the letter itself.

Finally, I have avoided the use of foreign or technical terms, no matter how established. Therefore, I have translated κοινόβιον as "monastic community" rather than leaving it as *coenobium*, in order also to distinguish it from μοναστήριον (*Letter* 390) and μονή (*Letter* 582), which I have translated as "monastery." The latter terms normally refer to the monastery as a site, as a collection of buildings or grounds, whereas the former term usually relates to the common life shared by the monks of the establishment. Either term may be adopted to include also the entire monastic complex or loose community of monks living either within or around the monastery proper, although the former term is more often used in this manner.

---

[51]The complete text will be published by Cistercian Publications, Kalamazoo MI.

Dates of the Desert Fathers

Agathon	d. 370
Ammoun	d. 350
Anthony	251–356
Arsenius	c.360–c.449
Athanasius of Alexandria	c.296–373
Augustine of Hippo	354–430
Barsanuphius	d.c. 543
Basil of Caesarea	330–379
Cyril of Scythopolis	fl.c. 524–558
Dorotheus of Gaza	c. 506-c. 570
Ephraim the Syrian	d. 373
Euthymius	376–473
Evagrius	c. 345–399
Hilarion	c. 291–c.371
Isaiah of Scetis	d.c. 489
Jerome	c. 341–420
John Cassian	360–435
John Chrysostom	347–407
John the Dwarf	c. 339–c. 407
John of Lycopolis	d. 395
John Moschos	7th century
John, the "Other Old Man"	d.c. 543
Macarius of Alexandria	293–393
Macarius of Egypt	c. 300–c. 390
Mark the Monk	5th century
Melanie the Elder	342–411

Melanie the Younger	380–c. 439
Moses the Ethiopian	d.c. 375
Nilus of Ancyra	5th century
Origen of Alexandria	185–c. 254
Pachomius	292–346
Palladius of Helenopolis	5th century
Pambo	304–373
Paul of Thebes	c. 235–c. 341
Paula the Elder	347–404
Paula the Younger	b.c. 397
Peter the Iberian	c. 409–c. 488
Poemen	d.c.450
Porphyry of Gaza	d. 420
Sabas	439–532
Serapion of Thmuis	d.c. 370
Seridos	d.c. 543
Silvanus	d.c. 412
Sisoes	d. 429
Symeon the Stylite	d. 459
Syncletica	380–c. 460
Theodore the Studite	759–826
Zeno, of Silvanus	d. 451
Zosimas (*Reflections*)	fl. 475–530

The Letters

TITLE

*Letters and Responses of two spiritual elders, named
Barsanuphius and John, who were living in silence near a
monastic community called that of Abba Seridos in the region
of Gaza, conveyed through that Abbot,[1] namely the same
Abba Seridos who also ministered to them.*

SUBTITLE

*Edifying teachings of St Barsanuphius and of John his disciple
and fellow-ascetic, which they conveyed through letters to the
brethren who inquired by way of Abba Seridos who ministered
to them and was the Abbot of the monastic community in
Gaza, where these holy elders lived in silence.*

PROLOGUE

How to read this book of letters

We entreat those who read this book to receive whatever is written
here with gratitude, reverence, and faith, and to endeavor especially
to arrive by the grace of God to the point of imitating the life and

---

[1]Throughout this selection, references to "Abbot" (with capitalized A) are to this
Seridos, by whose name the monastery became known in the region.

actions of those who spoke these words. For having trained their own life over a long period of time through endurance and faith according to God, and having according to the holy Apostle struggled "lawfully" (2 Tim 2.5), in all things following the way of the holy fathers, they became worthy of such great gifts from God.

However, as we are about to read this book, we are obliged to know that some of these words were spoken to hermits, others to monks in community, others to those in choir, and yet others to priests and Christ-loving laypersons. Again some were intended for younger monastics or novices, others for those already advanced in age and disciplined in their habits, and others to those approaching the perfection of virtue—according to the capacity that each was able to hear the words.

Indeed, not all the same teachings are suitable for everyone. Just as in the ages of the body, there are different foods for the breast-feeding child, for the adolescent, and for the elderly, so also happens in the case of the spiritual stages. Often, these elders responded to questions bearing in mind the weakness of the thoughts in the persons inquiring, discreetly condescending to their level in order that those asking may not fall into despair, like we find in the *Lives of the Old Men*. So we must not receive as a general rule the words spoken in a loving way to particular people for the sake of their weakness. Rather, we should immediately discern that the response was surely addressed by the saints to the questioner in a personal way. For it may happen that such persons will one day come to their senses by the prayers of the saints, and thus come to a condition appropriate for monks, and then will again hear what is of benefit to them.

I entreat you in the Lord to remember also my humble person in your holy prayers. For I have by God's help transmitted here in writing these responses for the benefit of those who read them with fear of God, so that the words of the saints may not be to me unto judgment, but that I may be protected by their prayers and yours, now and to the day of judgment. Amen.

QUESTIONS AND RESPONSES

Memory and inspiration

1. *Response* from the Great Old Man to Abba John of Beersheba,[2] who asked to come and live with them in the monastic community.

It is written in the Apostle: "The one who has begun a good work in you will himself also complete it until the day of our Lord Jesus Christ" (Phil 1.6). And again our Master said to him who approached him: "If any person does not renounce everything," including one's family, "and hate one's own soul too, that person cannot be my disciple" (Lk 14.33, 26). It is possible for God to inform us about the verse: "Behold, it is a good and pleasing thing for brothers to dwell together in the same place" (Ps 132.1). I pray that you will attain the measure that is written in Acts, that "as many as had properties sold them, and brought the price of what was sold and laid it at the Apostles' feet" (Acts 4.34).

Knowing your intention that is according to God, I said to our beloved son, Seridos, who after God protects us from people—and we hope to God that he will also protect you together with us: "Receive our brother John with much love, and do not hesitate at all. For, two years ago, God revealed to me that he would be coming here, and that many brothers would be gathering around us, but I kept this revelation until I learned precisely what the Lord is doing. Now, then, that the time is fulfilled, I have also declared it to you." And since you have reckoned that I should provide you with something that I wear, behold, in the presence of the brother, I have removed the cowl from my head and sent it with him to you, saying: "Give it to him, and bring me another in its place." Keep it then until the end of your life. For it will protect you from many evil things and

---

[2] *Letters* 1–54 are addressed to this John, mostly by Barsanuphius, with the exception of *Letter* 3.

trials. Do not give it to anyone else. Indeed, it is a blessing of God from my hands. Strive to complete your work, and to be acquitted of all things, just as we have; and settle with us, carefree, dedicating your time to God.

And I, Seridos, tell you something else wonderful. As the Old Man said this, I thought to myself: "How can I remember these things in order to write them down? Had the Old Man wanted, I could have brought here the ink and paper, heard his words one by one, and written them down." But he knew what I was thinking, and his face shone like fire, and he said to me: "Go on, write; do not be afraid. Even if I tell you ten thousand words, the Spirit of God will not let you write one letter too much or too little. And not because you so wish, but because it is guiding your hand to write in a coherent manner."

Give thanks to God

6. Letter from the same Great Old Man written to the same Abba John when he was carrying out certain duties in his country for the monastic community, and was disturbed by bodily warfare.

Write the following words to our brother. While you are still outside carrying out your labor according to your ability for the sake of God and for the souls of the brothers, or rather for the sake of our and your rest and silence—for if the brothers find rest and protection through us, we too find perfect silence through them, and the written word is fulfilled in us: "A brother aided by a brother is like a strong and fortressed city" (Prov 18.19)—do away with all the relationships and pretexts that you may have while you are still outside, and do not allow any occasion or relation with any person, which may draw you backward. If you do not do this, you will not be able to live in perfect silence. For, this is how we have also lived. Therefore, if you do this, I hope that your silence will be perfect. Indeed, your lot is surely with us, and your portion is with us forever.

Let no one learn yet what we are writing to you. So when you perform your labor, if the work prospers in your eyes, give thanks to God and pray to him. Indeed, this is what is meant by: "In everything give thanks" (1 Thess 5.18). And let us not neglect to render thanks to God, like the one about whom you once told the parable that he used to go and pray in church in order that food might be secured for him. Then he met someone who said: "Have breakfast with me today, and then go pray," but he replied: "I am not going to come; for that is what I was going to ask from God in prayer." But whether we find what we want or not, we should offer prayer and thanks to God. And see that you bear "the dying of Jesus in your body" (2 Cor 4.10) through everything.

Rejoice in the Lord

10. *Response* from the Great Old Man to the same person, when a stone fell on his foot and caused him much pain and disheartenment.

To our beloved brother John, convey greetings in the Lord. According to your bodily labor for our sake, and the crushing of your spirit for the sake of God, may the Master God fill your soul, my beloved one, one hundredfold with heavenly blessings. Understand what I am writing to you, brother, and conceal it within you. I shall make you hear a heavenly joy from our divine Master. In the name of the Holy Trinity, I find that you are a co-heir of the gifts that I have been given by God. And I expect that step–by–step you will quickly achieve them. For it is possible for a person to reach the point of rest quickly as a result of ascetic labor. Again it is possible for another person to reach this on account of humility. And I hope that you will have both of these, as wrath dies in you when anger is choked from your heart. Then the written word will be fulfilled in you: "Look upon my humility and my labor, and forgive all my sins" (Ps 24.18).

And since I said that you will achieve these gifts step by step, look at the Gospels, how—and how often—Christ gave gifts to the disciples, whether for healing or for casting out demons, telling them of the final perfection in regard to the forgiveness of sins: "Whosesoever sins you forgive, they are forgiven" (Jn 20.23). Therefore, if on account of your labor for the sake of God, your sins are forgiven, this is precisely the measure that I want you to attain. If you read in this letter any words that are difficult to understand, ask Seridos, who is at one with your soul and my beloved son, and he will explain to you the difficult passages through the grace of God. For I have prayed to God for him about this matter.

You then, as a man of God, should unceasingly run the way that is prepared for you, so that you may reach with joy the harbor of Christ that we have reached, and hear the voice that is full of joy, light, life, and gladness, saying to you: "Well done, good and faithful servant; you have been faithful over a few things, I will set you over many things; enter into the joy of your Lord" (Mt 25.21). Rejoice in the Lord; rejoice in the Lord; rejoice in the Lord. May the Lord guard your soul and body from every evil, and from every opposition of the devil and every troubling imagination. The Lord will be your light, your protection, your way, your strength, your crown of gladness and eternal help. Pay attention to yourself. For, it is written: "Even what goes out from my lips, I will not put aside" (Ps 88.35).

The inner disposition

17. *Question* by the same person[3] to the same Great Old Man: I know, father, that these things occur to me because of my sins, and that I am senseless and the cause of evil. Yet, the one who brings me to this distress is the Abbot, because he is neglectful and overlooks things. So they are destroyed on account of him, and I cannot bear this. What should I do? For, I respond to these thoughts and do not

[3]John of Beersheba.

receive any strength to deal with them. And forgive me, that "once I have spoken, but I shall not add to it a second time" (Job 39.35). But I marvel at how that warmth of my love for the Abbot and the brothers has grown cold. Pray for me for the Lord's sake.

Response

Brother, remember that the Lord told his disciples: "Are you also without understanding?" (Mt 15.16 and Mk 7.18) For I wrote to you saying: "Be accurate with your thoughts." If you had toiled to be accurate, you would have learned that the essence of what you have just written to me I first wrote to you, and there was no need for me to write again. Nevertheless, I shall tell you more in regard to your questions. First, however, I shall rebuke you. You called yourself a sinner, but in your deeds you did not consider yourself as such. For one who considers oneself a sinner and the cause of evil is neither contentious nor angry against anyone else, but considers everyone to be better and wiser than oneself.

Now, if your thoughts ridicule you, telling you that you are such a person, then how do they move your heart against those who are better than you? Be careful, brother; you are not saying the truth. For we have still not reached the point of considering ourselves sinners. If anyone loves the person who rebukes him, that person is wise. But if anyone says that he loves, yet does not do what he hears from that person, then this is actually hatred. If you are a sinner, why do you blame and accuse your neighbor, claiming that he causes your distress? Do you not know that each person is tempted by one's own conscience, and this brings distress? This is what I wrote to you about the brothers, that "they should not make a gnat into a camel" (Mt 23.24), and so on. Pray, rather, that you may be sharers in the fear of God.

As for calling yourself senseless, do not deceive yourself, but search and you will find that it is not so. If you believe that you are, then you would not become angry, since you would be unable to discern whether things are right or wrong. For a senseless person is called foolish. And a senseless, foolish person implies a person lacking salt. And how can a person lacking salt season and salt others? See, brother, how we are mocked and speak only with our mouth, but our deeds show us to be otherwise. However, when we respond to our thoughts, we do not receive any strength, because first we accept to criticize our neighbor, and so the strength of our spirit is weakened, and we blame our brother when we ourselves are at fault.

If you claim that everything depends on "God who shows mercy" and "not on the one who wills or runs" (Rom 9.16), then why do you not understand and love your brother with all your heart, in perfect love? How many have desired to follow us elders, and ran, but could not attain this? And when our brother came to the monastery, God sent us to him, and made him our true child. For God loves the inner disposition.

As for your claim, that "I have spoken once" (Job 39.35), and so on, if you are fighting to win, then you are blessed. For it is not granted to all. And as for the other thoughts, refer every thought to God. Say: "God knows what is best," and you will find rest, and your strength to endure will gradually return.

Do not completely cease speaking. However, if you do speak and are not heard, nor find favor in your words, do not be sad; for this is rather to your benefit. In regard to the things that you admire, perfect love is without failing (1 Cor 13.8), and one who obtains it remains in its warmth, enclosed in love toward God and neighbor. However, as for the prayers that you recently wrote, you ought to be satisfied with the promise that I gave you; I am praying ceaselessly to God for you night and day. So this too was unnecessary for you to write. Therefore, you have divine food from me for a long time. Persevere, and wait patiently for the Lord, in Christ Jesus our Lord. To him be the glory to the ages. Amen.

On tears

18. *Response* from the same Great Old Man to the same person[4] when he asked whence the warmth, coldness, and hardness of heart come about, as well as about bodily warfare.

On warmth and coldness, it is clear that the Lord has been called "fire" (Deut 4.24; Heb 12.29), warming and burning "the hearts and loins" (Ps 7.9; 25.2). If it is so, then the devil is cold, and all coldness comes from him. For if it were not so, how then is it said, that "then the love of many will grow cold" (Mt 24.12)? What else does the word "then" signify, but "the times of the adversary? Therefore, if we feel coldness, let us call upon God, and he will come and warm our heart in his perfect love, not only toward him but also toward our neighbor. And the face of his warmth will banish the coldness of that hater of good.

Now if the fountain of your heart's tears has been dried up, and your underbelly has been moistened, nevertheless continue to feast the Lord "in your house" (Lk 19.5) and he will dry up the latter, purifying the fountain of your tears for the flowing of spiritual[5] water. Anyone who wishes to come to the fear of God, does so through patience. For it says: "I waited patiently for the Lord, and he gave heed to me and heard my prayer. . . ." What else does he say? "And he raised me from the pit of wretchedness, and from the miry clay" (Ps 39.1–2). It is from such a pit that hardness of heart is also thought to come. If this is what you desire, then obtain it and you will be saved in Christ Jesus our Lord.

The rule of ascesis

23. *Question* by the same brother[6] to the same Great Old Man: I ask you, father and teacher, not to be angry with my faults, but to give

[4]John of Beersheba.
[5] Lit. "noetic."
[6]John of Beersheba.

me a rule, as to how I must behave in fasting, psalmody, and prayer; and tell me whether I should make any distinction between the various days.

Response

Brother, if you had paid attention to the words of your questions, you would have understood the power of wisdom. If I am your father and teacher, why do you want me to be angry? For a father is compassionate, having no wrath at all. And a teacher is long-suffering and foreign to wrath. Now, as for the rule about which you inquired, you are going around in endless circles in order to "enter by the narrow gate into life" eternal (Mt 7.13). Behold, Christ tells you precisely how you must enter. Leave aside the rules of people, and listen to him saying: "The one who endures to the end will be saved" (Mt 10.22; 24.13; Mk 13.13). Therefore, if one does not have endurance, one will not enter into life.

So do not look for a command. I do not want you to be "under the law but under grace" (Rom 6.14). For it is said: "The law is not made for the righteous person" (1 Tim 1.9). Keep discretion, like a helmsman steering the boat according to the winds. And when you are sick, act accordingly in all things, just as you have written; and when you are well, act again accordingly. Because when the body too is unwell, it does not receive food normally. Thus, the ascetic rule proves useless in this regard too. And as far as the days are concerned, treat them all as equal, holy, and good. So do everything with understanding, and it will prove for you unto life in Christ Jesus our Lord. To him be the glory to the ages. Amen.

Endurance of trials

31. They[7] went about a great deal in Egypt before finding handiwork, and they endured great tribulation and distraction in many

---

[7]That is, members of the monastic community.

ways, and so weariness came upon him. Since the Great Old Man foresaw this spiritually, he prepared the following response for him:[8]

My child, write down what I am saying, or rather what God is saying, and prepare to give this letter to brother John. First, greetings in the Lord. Afterward, tell him: Why do you grow weary in your tribulations, like a man of flesh, as if you had not heard that tribulations await you, as the Spirit also said to Paul (Acts 20.23), who also comforted those who were with him in the boat to rejoice (Acts 27.21–26 and 33–36)? Do you not know that "the tribulations of the righteous are many" (Ps 33.19), and that they are tested through these like gold? If we are righteous, let us be proved in tribulation. And if we are sinners, let us endure them as deserving. For, "patience works proof" (Rom 5.4).

Let us call to mind all of the saints from the beginning in order to see what they endured. For while they did good and spoke good and stood entirely by the truth, yet they were hated and afflicted by people to their very end. Still, they "would pray for their enemies and for those who despised" (Lk 6.28; Mt 5.44) them, in accordance with the Savior's words. Have you then also been sold like the honorable Joseph (Gen 37), and have your "hands served in the basket" (Ps 80.6), and have you been lowered into two pits (Gen 37.24 and 40.15)? Or have you been badly treated like Moses from childhood to old age (Heb 11.25)? What have you endured, slothful one? Have you been persecuted and envied like David by Saul, or by your own son unto death, having to mourn for him when he died (2 Sam 1.11–27 and 18.13)? Or have you been thrown into the sea like Jonah (Jon 1.15)?

Lazy and beloved one, why is your thought growing faint? Do not fear or dread like a coward, lest you fall short of God's promises (Heb 4.1). Do not be terrified like an unbeliever, but give courage to your thoughts of little faith. Love your tribulations in all things, so that you may become an approved son of the saints. Remember "the

---

[8]John of Beersheba.

patience of Job" (Jas 5.11) and those who followed him, and be zealous in following their footsteps. Remember the dangers, tribulations, bonds, hungers, and multitude of other evils that Paul
endured (cf. 2 Cor 11.24–27), and say to your faintheartedness: "I am
a stranger to you." Remember what I wrote to you: "Whether the
matter at hand prospers or not, render thanks to God." Understand
how worldly things are, that they are corruptible and transitory,
whereas patience according to God saves the person who has
obtained it.

Behold, you are struggling to bring and to perform handiwork.
In order, therefore, that I may show you the Apostolic word, that
"this does not depend on the one that wills, nor on the one that runs,
but on God who is merciful" (Rom 9.16), behold God is sending you
people who have need of the world. When you receive them, do not
say that I said anything about them, lest they be tempted by vainglory. Love them as genuine brothers, and make your thought give
rest to their thought. For they despise the world, desiring to save
their souls. And through me, God—I am now writing out of fore-
knowledge—is drawing them here to you, in order for you to learn
that they have entirely despised it. Therefore, brother, hold my hand
and walk in the "straight and narrow way that leads to life" eternal
(Mt 7.14), in our Lord Jesus Christ, to whom is the glory to the ages.
Amen.

Physical and spiritual illness

35. *Response* from the same Great Old Man to the same person[9]
when he asked about brothers with physical illness, and about others with spiritual illness, whether he should take them in himself;
and whether he should tell the Abbot to relieve the novices a little
from the vigil; and also about his long silence.

[9]John of Beersheba.

Brother, the response to the three thoughts is one—do not force the will, but only sow "in hope" (1 Cor 9.10). For our Lord too did not force anyone, but only preached the Gospel; and whosoever wanted, listened. I know that you know that I am neither neglecting nor despising your love. But this tolerance is for the best. For when we pray, and God is long-suffering in his response, he does this for our best interest, in order that we may learn long-suffering and not grow faint, saying that we prayed but were not heard. For God knows what is best for us. Rejoice in the Lord, my brother, and be carefree from all, and pray for me, my beloved soul-mate.[10]

Leave the worldly and long for the heavenly

37. A Christ-loving layperson sent a question to the same Abba John about some matter, and was given an answer. And when John regretted what he had said in response, he informed the same Great Old Man, saying: "Forgive me, for I am drunk and do not know what I am doing."

I tell you often: "Let the dead bury their dead" (Mt 8.22; Lk 9.60), and instead you are not even yet disgusted by their foul smell. Look at what you are saying. You do not know what you are saying. Indeed, a drunk person is ridiculed by people, is beaten, despised, does not account himself worthy, offers no opinions, teaches no one, gives no advice about anything, cannot discern between what is good and what is wrong. If you speak with your mouth, and show otherwise with your deeds, then you are speaking in ignorance.

Do not fall asleep, lest you suddenly hear: "Behold the bridegroom. Go out to meet him" (Mt 25.6). And where will your response then be: "I am busy"? He has made you carefree, and you do not want this; he has removed from you every worry, and you entangle yourself; he has given you rest, and you wish to toil. There is no time for you to mourn and weep for your sins. Remember how

[10]Lit. "of the same soul."

he told you that the door will be shut (Mt 25.10). Hurry, so that you do not remain outside with the foolish virgins. Pass over with your thought from this vain world to another age. Leave the worldly, and long for the heavenly. Abandon the corruptible, and you shall find the incorruptible. In your mind, flee from the temporary, and you shall arrive at the eternal. Die completely, that you may live completely in Christ Jesus our Lord, to whom be the glory to the ages. Amen.

Do not fear temptation

39. *Response* from the same Great Old Man to the same brother[11] when he wanted to cut off conversation even with his own attendant because he was told to be carefree in order to approach the city where the monastery was located. He also asked about his thought that was seeking the causes of the temptations rising up against him in various ways.

Say the following to this brother: Wait a little longer. For it is not yet time. Indeed I care for you more so than you do yourself; or rather, God takes care of you. Brother John, do not be at all afraid of the temptations that rise up against you in order to test you. Indeed, the Lord will not surrender you to them. Therefore, whenever something like this comes upon you, do not labor in seeking to investigate matters, but cry the name of Jesus, saying: "Jesus, help me," and he will hear you; for "he is near those who call upon him" (Ps 144.18). Do not be faint-hearted, but run willingly and you shall obtain (cf. 1 Cor 9.24), in Christ Jesus our Lord, to whom be the glory.

[11]John of Beersheba.

Hold on to the Beloved

45. *Response* by the same Great Old Man to the same brother,[12] when he fell into great illness and was overcome by a very high fever, able neither to eat nor to sleep for many days, and—being influenced by the devil—he cried out insulting the Abbot as well as the brothers attending him.

Brother, how is it that your heart has been watered down, to leave the Beloved and run after the enemy? You have left the voice of the Shepherd Christ, and have followed after the wolf devil. What has happened to you? What have you endured? What are these cries, which the Apostle has numbered among things of ill repute, saying: "Let every cry and blasphemy and wrath be taken from you, together with every evil" (Eph 4.31)? Nothing has happened to you beyond your strength, as the Apostle cries aloud: "God is faithful, and will not allow us to be tried beyond our strength" (1 Cor 10.13), and so forth. Awaken from this turmoil of evil thoughts, and take up the staff of the Cross, with which you will drive away the wolves, namely the demons, and remember to say: "Why are you so downcast, my soul, and why do you so trouble me? Have hope in God, and I shall give thanks to him; he is the salvation of my countenance and my God" (Ps 41.6, 12 and 42.5).

Therefore, be sober from now on, and do not be consumed like a foolish child that has no perception. Since you ought to ascend the Cross with Christ, and to be nailed with the nails and pierced with the spear, why do you carry on, poor wretch, and cry out with force against Christ and with insults against your brothers? Where is for you the phrase: "Give preference to one another in honor" (Rom 12.10)? Enough for now. For it says: "Give occasion to a wise person and he shall become wiser" (Prov 9.9). Endure and be silent, and give thanks for all things. For so it says: "Give thanks in all things" (1 Thess 5.18)—which clearly means both "in necessities and in

[12]John of Beersheba.

afflictions" (2 Cor 6.4), and in illnesses and respites alike. Hold, therefore, on to God, and he will stay with you, and give you strength in his name; for his is the glory to the ages.

Christ's chastening and rebuke

48. When the Abbot[13] delayed for some reason in bringing him[14] the above reply, he blamed him strongly, causing the former great disheartenment. And when some of the brothers, who were being attended to for their sickness, spoke to him about certain matters which were being done idly and unprofitably in the monastic community, instead of admonishing and correcting them for such slander, he said that these things do not please him either. And when the Abbot later told him: "I did this according to the advice of the Old Man," he replied: "The Old Man lets you walk according to your own will." Upon hearing this, the Great Old Man sent him the following response, pointing out to him that "those things which seem to us not to be happening correctly are being done by economy, and are beyond our comprehension."

Again love arouses us after some time to strike you with the rod of Christ's chastening and rebuke, in order that the Scriptural word may also be fulfilled in us, that: "The wounds of a friend are more trustworthy" (Prov 27.6), and so forth. And again, if we chasten you, do not grow faint, remembering the proverb that says: "My son, do not despise the chastening of the Lord, nor grow faint when you are reproved by him. Indeed, the Lord chastens whom he loves, and scourges every child that he receives" (Prov 3.11–12). Even if I rebuke you, you are not ignorant of the words of the Apostle: "Reprove, rebuke, exhort" (2 Tim 4.2).

Where is your mind, slothful one? Where does your thought dwell, lazy one? Why is it that the lords of your mind contradict

[13]Seridos.
[14]John of Beersheba.

within you the disciples of the Master, that you should not accept him to mount your mind as your Master and to enter Jerusalem (Lk 19.33–35), casting out of the temple of God "those who sell and buy" (Mt 21.12; Mk 11.15) and putting to shame the Scribes and the Pharisees? Why is it that, when you ought to dwell in Jerusalem, they drag you to Babylon? Why do you leave the water of Siloam (Is 8.6), and wish to drink from the murky waters of the Egyptians? Why do you move away from the way of humility, which says: "Who am I ? (2 Sam 7.18; 1 Chron 17.16 and 29.14) I am but earth and ashes (Gen 18.27; Job 42.6)," and wish to walk the corrupt way which is filled with trials and dangers?

Where have you cast my words, spoken to you day and night? Where is it that I have asked you, as if talking to myself, to head, and where do you see yourself heading? Where do I want you to be, and where are you on account of your uncontrolled tongue, which you release at random? And if you give thought to your neighbor, are you not being scrupulous in your understanding, especially to the one who protects us after God, and lays down his own neck for us? Instead, we ought to thank him and pray that he might be preserved from every evil for the benefit of us and of many others, learning this from the holy Apostle, who gave thanks for some saying: "They laid down their own necks for my sake" (Rom 16.4)?

So what is it that you do not remember? The freedom from care, which God granted you through him? Or the relaxation which you share in silence as a king, while he bears the weight of those things that come to and go from us, leaving us undisturbed? For if they come because of us, it is we who ought to bear their care, and not he. Therefore, I owe many thanks to God who gave us a genuine son according to our soul, just as God willed. And in return for this, you told him senselessly: "I have washed my hands of you." In fact, you did this not once but many times, drowning his soul in much sorrow, and failing to remember the Apostle who said: "Lest such a person be swallowed by greater sorrow" (2 Cor 2.7).

Were it not for the hand of God and the prayer of his fathers, his heart would have been shattered. Where are my commandments to you, to "weep, mourn, not seek to be accounted for, and to measure yourself in nothing"? I am drawing your love toward another direction. Pass over from the world, and henceforth mount the Cross, be lifted from the earth. "Shake the dust from your feet" (Mt 10.14). "Despise shame" (Heb 12.2). Do not join the Chaldeans in kindling the furnace, so that you may not be burned with them (Dan 3.23) by God's wrath. Hold every person "as being superior to yourself" (Phil 2.3). "Weep for your corpse" (Sir 22.11; Jn 11.31). "Cast out your beam" (Mt 7.5). Rebuild your house, which was destroyed. Cry out: "Have mercy on me, son of David, that I may see again" (Mk 10.47–51; Lk 18.38–41). Learn, so "that every mouth may be sealed" (Rom 3.19), "and do not speak boastfully" (Ob 12). "Shut your door" (Is 26.20) against the enemy. "Hold your words in balance, and make a bar for your door" (Sir 28.25).

You know how I speak to you. Understand my words. Labor to scrutinize them and you will find godly treasures hidden in them. Make them bring forth fruits worthy of God. And do not put to shame my gray hair as I pray for you day and night. May the Lord grant you to understand and act in his fear. Amen.

And since you told him: "The Old Man lets you walk according to your own will," then I shall bear alone the judgment of which the Lord spoke through the Prophet: "Truly I say to you, if you see your brother walking in a way that is not good, and you do not tell him that this way is evil, I shall require his blood from your hand (Ezek 3.18 and 33.8)." Do not be ridiculed, but believe the Apostle who says: "We shall give account" (Heb 13.17) for him. Yet you do not understand what is even happening.

Ruminate on my letters

49. Having thanked the Old Man[15] for the correction, he[16] begged him to write to him often about the salvation of his soul. Similarly, he entreated the Great Old Man to tell him about a thought that he sought to tell the Abbot.

Brother John, I do not know what this is. I have written to you from A to Z, from the beginner's stage to that of perfection, from the outset of the way to its very end, from the "putting off of the old man with earthly desires" (Eph 4.22; Col 3.9) to the "putting on of the new man created according to God" (Eph 4.24; Col 3.10), from becoming estranged from the sensible world to becoming a citizen of heaven and an inheritor of the spiritual land of promises. Ruminate on my letters, and you will be saved. In these, you have the Old and the New Testaments, if you are able to understand. And if you understand them, you will have no need of any other book.

Shake off forgetfulness, and move away from darkness, so that your heart may be at peace with your senses, and all this will come to you. Let the smoke of the idol sacrifices from your spiritual Nineveh disappear, and the fragrance from the incense of your spiritual repentance will spread throughout its streets, preventing the wrath which was threatening destruction (Jon 3).

Why are you sleeping? Why are you using the responses for your salvation as pillows, when they are for the salvation of those who study them with faith? Stop dreaming; wake up from your deep sleep. Quicken your pace. Take over Zoar, so that the destruction of the five cities may not overtake you (Gen 19.22). Do not turn backward, in order not to become a pillar of salt (Gen 19.26). Become "wise as the serpent" (Gen 3.1; Mt 10.16), so that your enemies may not lead you astray; but be "harmless like the doves" (Mt 10.16), so that requital may not war against you. Become a genuine servant of one master, otherwise you will be enslaved to many. Do not separate

[15]Barsanuphius.
[16]John of Beersheba.

yourself from him. For the unfaithful servant received judgment for this. Watch even how you sit. Say to yourself: "Why am I sitting like this? What have I gained from this sitting?" And the loving God will enlighten your heart to understand.

Behold, now he has made you carefree from every earthly concern. Give heed to yourself, and watch where you are and what you want, and God will assist you in everything, my brother. And as for the thought that you asked me to tell my son, I could of course tell him, but unless you tell him with your own mouth, you are estranging yourself from genuine and perfect love toward him. If you are one soul and one heart, according to Scripture (Acts 4.32), then no one hides anything from one's heart. Wake up to yourself, for you are still heavy-hearted. The Lord will forgive you.

Cast your concerns on God

72. An old man who was ill, named Andrew,[17] who was living in silence in the monastic community, declared some of his secret faults to the same Great Old Man, while at the same time giving thanks for the fact that he had been counted worthy to dwell near such a man; he also asked about his bodily illness.

Response by Barsanuphius

If you truly believe that it is actually God who has brought you to this place, then entrust him with your cares and cast on him all your concerns; and he will dispose your affairs as he wills. However, if you hold back from him in regard to any matter, whether about some bodily illness or the passions of the soul, then you are obliged to deal with these as you know. For double-mindedness, after a person has left everything to God, always brings that person to say, if one is a

---

[17]Andrew, an elderly and ill brother, is the recipient of *Letters* 72 to 123.

little afflicted: "If perhaps I had taken care of my body, I would not have to be afflicted in this way."

Therefore, the person who gives oneself to God must do so unto death and with one's whole heart. God knows, far more than we do, what is good for our soul and body. And to the degree that he allows you to be afflicted in the body, he accordingly lightens the burden of your sins. God, then, demands nothing from you but thanksgiving and patience and prayer for the forgiveness of sins.

See how proud I am, that while I am ridiculed by the demons, thinking that I have love according to God, I am overcome to tell you: "I now bear half of your burden; and in the future God is again able to help you." I have spoken as someone who is insane. For, I know that I am weak and incapable and naked of every good work. Yet my shamelessness does not allow me to despair. For I have a compassionate master, one who is merciful and loving, who stretches out his hand to a sinner until his last breath. Cleave unto him, and in every matter he will do "beyond what we ask or imagine" (Eph 3.20). To him be the glory to the ages. Amen. Forgive me, my brother, and pray for me.

I bear your burden

73. Having heard this from him, namely the words: "I bear half of your burden," grieving that he did not promise him complete forgiveness, he entreated and implored him a second time, that through Christ he might grant him this completely.

Response by Barsanuphius

I admire your love, brother, but you do not understand the affairs of love that is according to God. In the first place, God knows how I regard myself as earth and ashes, being nothing at all. But if I say something to someone beyond my measure, or beyond my power,

I speak moved by the love of Christ, knowing—as I said—that I am
nothing but a useless servant.

Since then you did not understand what I told you, namely that
I bear half your sins, I have made you a partner with me. For I did
not say to you: "I bear one-third," leaving you to bear more and be
burdened more than I. And again, I said what I have said in order to
banish self-love; this is why I did not speak to you of bearing two-
thirds, showing myself to be stronger than you; for such conduct
would be vainglory. And I did not say: "I bear the whole." This
belongs to the perfect, to those who have become brothers of Christ,
who laid down his own life for our sake, and who loved those who
have loved us with perfect love in order to do this.

Again, I would have rendered you a stranger to spiritual labor if
I had not spoken in this way. So I am not vainglorious, in order to
ascribe to myself the whole; nor am I envious, by making you a partner in this good conversion. If we are brothers, let us share equally
in our Father's property, and injustice will not divide us. However, if
you wish to cast on me the whole burden, then for the sake of obedience I accept this too. Forgive me that great love leads me to talking nonsense. Yet may it be to you for gladness in Christ Jesus our
Lord, to whom be the glory to the ages. Amen.

Let us endure

74. Request from the same person to the same Great Old Man, that
he might pray for him on account of an illness that befell on him.

Response by Barsanuphius[18]

Scripture says: "We have passed through fire and water, and you lead

---

[18]This letter is quoted by Gregory the Sinaite in the fourteenth century. See his
treatise *On Silence and the Two Methods of Prayer* PG 150.1317. See *Orientalia Christiana* 9.2 (Rome, 1927), 163. The *Correspondence* of Barsanuphius and John was also
influential on later Hesychast writers, especially through its emphasis on silence (see
Letters 8–9, 163, 565, and 582) and prayer (see *Letters* 89, 124, 421, and 827).

us out to refreshment" (Ps 65.12). Those who wish to please God must pass through certain afflictions. How can we call the holy martyrs blessed for the sufferings they endured for the sake of God, if we are unable to bear a mere fever? Say to your afflicted soul: "Is not a fever better for you than the fire of hell?" Let us not despair during illness, for the Apostle said: "When I am weak, then I am strong" (2 Cor 12.10). Observe how "God directs hearts and reins" (Ps 7.9). Let us endure, let us bear, let us become disciples of the Apostle who says: "patience in tribulation" (Rom 12.12). Let us give thanks to God in all things, that the saying may not be fulfilled in us too: "he will give thanks to you, after you have done good to him" (Ps 48.19).

And if you required bodily care, or for the sake of your testing have found a little tribulation, why do you not remember Job's words: "If we have received good things from the hand of God, shall we not endure the bad things?" (Job 2.10) Notice how those who in all things desire comfort shall hear: "In your lifetime, you enjoyed good things" (Lk 16.25). Let us not slacken. For we have a merciful God, who knows our weakness better than we. And if in testing us he brings on us illness, we nevertheless have the Apostle offering us some padding and saying: "God is faithful, and will not allow you to be tempted beyond your ability, but will together with the temptation also show you the way out, so that you may endure it" (1 Cor 10.13).

The Lord will strengthen the weak person alike and those who serve that person; and both these tasks will be for the glory of God. Look to the end of your patience, and do not grow despondent or weary. For God is nearby, saying: "I shall not leave you nor forsake you" (Heb 13.5). Believe me, brothers, for vainglory has gained control over me. Never have I in sickness laid down to rest or put down my handiwork; and yet great illnesses have come to me. Recently vainglory has been tricky, ever since I have entered this cell, and it does not allow illness to come to me. And I am grieved, because I desire patience, and I do not know what I can endure. No affliction comes my way, and I melt when I hear: "Whoever endures to the end will be saved" (Mt 10.22). Pray that I may remain holding the hope of salvation in Christ Jesus our Lord, to whom be the glory. Amen.

Illness as a substitute for fasting

78. *Question* from the same brother to the same Great Old Man: Since I have severe rheumatism in my feet and hands, and fear that it might come from the demons, tell me father if this is so, and what I should do. For, I am greatly in distress, being unable to fast, and being compelled to consume food many times. And what does it mean, when I see wild beasts in my dream? I entreat you, master, for the Lord's sake, to send me a small blessing from your holy food and drink, that I may receive comfort from them.

Response by Barsanuphius

Do not grieve, my beloved one. For this is not from the demons, as you think, but it is an external draft, a discipline from God for our improvement, so that we may give thanks to God. Was not Job a genuine friend of God? And what did he not endure, giving thanks and blessing to God? And the end of his patience led him to incomparable glory. Therefore, you also should be a little patient, and you will see the glory of God.

As for fasting, do not grieve. For as I have already told you, God does not require of anyone beyond their ability. What else is fasting but discipline of the body, in order to enslave a healthy body and weaken it on account of the passions? For he says: "When I am weak, then I am strong" (2 Cor 12.10). However, illness is greater than discipline, and is reckoned as a substitute for ascetic behavior; and this is even truer of the person who endures it with patience and gives thanks to God. That person reaps the fruit of salvation from such patience.

Therefore, instead of the body being weakened through fasting, it is weakened in and of itself. Give thanks that you have been exempted from the toil of regular behavior. So, if you eat ten times, do not grieve, for you are not condemned. For this is neither a result of demonic action, nor of slack thought; but it is happening to us in order to test and benefit the soul.

As far as the dreams about wild beasts, they are demonic fantasies, which want to deceive you through these, in order to make you believe that your suffering comes from the demons. However, "the Lord abolishes them by the word of his mouth" (2 Thess 2.8) through the prayers of the saints. Amen.

And do not grieve. "For whom the Lord loves he chastens, and he scourges every child whom he receives" (Heb 12.6 [Prov 3.12]). Yet I also believe in regard to this bodily suffering that God will do with you as his mercy wills. May the Lord strengthen you and establish you in order to endure. Amen. I have sent you a little water from the vessel of our blessed father, Euthymius. I have also sent you a small blessing from my own food, so that you may bless my food. Pray for me, dearest one.

Illness and ascesis

79. *Question* from the same person to the Other Old Man. Pray for my most unbearable illness, father, and declare to me about diet, whether it does not perhaps cause a scandal that I readily and continually eat. And tell me about chanting the Psalms, what I must do. For I have no strength to recite the Psalms. Plant me, master, and water me (cf. 1 Cor 3.6–8); reveal to me whether that which our holy father has said, namely that: "The Lord will work his mercy with you," referred to my death.

Response by John

Although I have kept silent, I did so because I had no word to speak, or anything good to offer you. But why do you ask bread of one who eats carobs? I am telling you this because, even though I am nothing, I congratulate you on what our blessed father wrote to you. Behold, then, he is offering you the solid food of spiritual bread. Why do you need my very watery milk, which only creates distaste? Neither Scripture nor the fathers have forbidden condescension toward the body, when it is brought about not by sensual pleasure but with discernment. Therefore when, as he has already told you, you eat and drink neither with waste nor with indulgence, then these do not bring condemnation to you or scandal upon others. For the Lord said about these: "They do not defile the human person" (Mt 15.11; Mk 7.15).

However, as far as psalmody and liturgy are concerned, do not be distressed. For God does not require these of you on account of your illness. One who gives heed to oneself is distressed in ascetic struggle for the sake of the Lord and for one's own salvation. You, then, have the affliction of illness in the place of distress through ascetic struggle. And about your illness, again do not grow weary. The Lord does not forsake you, but allows the illness for your interest, as he knows best, so that you may not be afflicted beyond your capacity.

Nevertheless, the Great Old Man was not speaking about your death at this time, but about the mercy that God will work within your love. So I beseech you to endure as he told you, and you will truly see the glory of God. In regard to the planting, if it is altogether true that "the one who plants and waters" (1 Cor 3.6–8) is nothing—and you have ascribed both of these to me—instead of me, who am nothing, you have "God who increases" and protects and works within you according to his mercy. Therefore, enjoying his goodness, "be courageous and strong" (Deut 31.6), and pray for me that his mercy may also come to me.

Redirecting the thoughts

86. *Question* from the same person to the same Old Man: How should one examine the thoughts? And how does one avoid the stage of captivity?

Response by Barsanuphius

The examination of one's thoughts follows this pattern: when a thought comes, you should pay attention to what it produces. Let me give you an example. Suppose that someone has insulted you, and your thought troubles you in the matter of responding. Say to your thought: "If I respond, I disturb him and he is grieved against me. Therefore, be a little patient, and it will pass." However, if our thought is not against some person, but thinks about evil by itself, then you must examine the thought and say: "Where is this thought of evil leading?" and your thought will cease. Do the same in regard to all your thoughts.

When the thought enters, examine it immediately and cut it short. As far as the stage of captivity is concerned, great vigilance is required. So, then, as the fathers have said, if this leads your intellect to fornication, you should lead it to sanctification. If it leads your intellect to gluttony, you should bring it to asceticism. If it leads your intellect to hatred, you should bring it to love; and so on, and so forth. Do not grieve, for you will find mercy, according to the promises that you have received. "For if we live, we live unto the Lord; and if we die, we die unto the Lord" (Rom 14.8).

On how to pray

87. *Question* from the same person to the same Great Old Man: Tell me, father, about unceasing prayer, and in what measure it is to be found, and whether I am obliged to have a rule.

Response by Barsanuphius

Rejoice in the Lord, brother; rejoice in the Lord, beloved; rejoice in the Lord, fellow heir. Unceasing prayer (cf. 1 Thess 5.17) is in accordance with the measure of dispassion. Then, the coming of the Spirit is known, and teaches us everything. If it teaches us everything, then it also teaches us about prayer. For the Apostle says: "We do not know how to pray as we should. But the Spirit itself intercedes for us with ineffable groanings" (Rom 8.26).

Therefore, what should I now say to you about the buildings of Rome, when you have not yet been there? A person living in silence, especially one that is bedridden, has no rule. Therefore, be rather like a person who eats and drinks as much as he pleases. Thus, when you happen to be reading, and you see compunction in your heart, read as much as you can. Do the same when you recite the Psalms. Hold on to thanksgiving and the prayer: "Lord have mercy," as much as you can. And do not be afraid. "For the gifts of God are without repentance" (Rom 11.29).

Everything happens for your benefit

105. *Response* by the same Great Old Man to the same person, when he grew weary before the temptations that assailed him.

My brother and soul-mate[19] Andrew, do not grow weary. For God has not forsaken you; nor will he forsake you. This is the Master's promise to our common father Adam, and it will not pass away: "You shall eat your bread in the sweat of your brow" (Gen 3.19). Just as he decreed for the outer man, so also does this apply to the inner man, so that in our asceticism we may cooperate with the prayers of the saints. Moreover, these prayers accomplish a great deal, so that one does not remain fruitless.

Therefore, just as gold is fired in the furnace and held by means

[19]Lit. "of one soul."

of tongs, being beaten into shape by the hammer and thereby being tested and proving acceptable for a royal diadem, so also a person—who is supported by the prayer of the saints, which is able to and indeed does accomplish a great deal—is fired by sorrow and beaten by temptation. If such person endures with thanksgiving, then that person is shown to be a child of the kingdom. Therefore, everything happens to you for your benefit, in order that you too may have boldness among the saints on account of your own toils. So, do not be ashamed to offer up the first-fruits of these toils. Do not add grief to yourself instead of spiritual joy. And trust in him who has made a promise; for he will fulfill it (cf. Heb 10.23 and 11.11). Brother, be strong in the Lord.

Jesus, our elder brother

109. The same elder was delivered of temptation through the prayers of the holy Old Man and his spiritual teaching. So, he sent a word of thanks to him.

Response by Barsanuphius

Let us render all glory to the God of glory; and let us sing to him unto the ages. Amen. For glory does not belong to us, but is only proper to his Son and his Holy Spirit. God has led your love to our frailty in order that we may be of assistance to one another, in his desire also to fulfill the Scripture that says: "A brother that is helped by a brother is stronger than a fortified city" (Prov 18.19). May our elder brother assist all of us, and I mean Jesus; for, he was well-pleased to make us all his brothers.

And so, we are his brothers and are praised by the angels for the kind of brother that we have, who is able to strengthen us, capable of dividing the spoils with us (Lk 11.22), a chief captain who can crush our enemies in war, a physician who can heal our passions, a general during time of peace in order to submit and set our inner man at peace with the outer man, a nurse who can nurture us with spiritual food, able to grant us life with his life, and mercy through his compassion, a king endowing us with royalty, and a God who deifies us.

Knowing, therefore, that everything lies in him, pray to him. "For he knows what we require even before we ask it of him" (Mt 6.8) and he will grant every request of your soul, if you do not stand as a hindrance. Always offer glory to him; for to him is due glory, to the ages. Amen. Pray for me, brother, that I may know my weakness and be humbled.

God loves you more

113. The same person asked the same Great Old Man about the same matter.

Response

Brother and beloved of my soul, Andrew, if you knew about the gift of God in the way that you should, then every hair on your head would be transformed into a mouth and you would be unable but to glorify and give thanks to him as is proper. Nevertheless, I believe that you are learning. And, as God himself knows, there is not a blink of the eye or a moment of time that I do not have you in my mind and in my prayer. And, if I love you so much, then the God who created you loves you still more. I beseech him to guide and direct you in accordance with his will. Thus, he is directing you for the benefit of your soul. If he should be long-suffering against you, yet he is multiplying the benefit of your soul. Therefore, sit and offer thanks to him for everything, reckoning yourself as nothing and believing that all you have been told will occur, in Christ Jesus our Lord. Amen.

The inner work of the heart

119. *Response* by the same Great Old Man to the same brother, when a thought was sown inside him that not abstaining from food was preventing him from reaching what had been promised.

It is not because I wish to abolish abstinence and the monastic discipline that I am always telling your love to perform the needs of your body as necessary—far be it from me! Rather, I am saying that, if the inner work does not come to our assistance after God, then one is laboring in vain on the outward man. For that is why the Lord said: "It is not the things that go into a person's mouth that defile that person, but the things that come out of the mouth" (Mt 15.11).

Indeed, inner work with labor of heart brings purity, and purity brings true quiet of heart, and such quiet brings humility, and humility renders a person the dwelling-place of God, and from this dwelling-place the evil demons are banished, together with the devil who is their captain, as well as their unworthy passions. Then, that person is found to be a temple of God, sanctified, illumined, purified, graceful, filled with every fragrance and goodness and gladness; and that person is found to be a God-bearer, or rather is even found to be a god, according to the one who said: "I have said, that you are gods, and all children of the Most High" (Ps 81.6 and Jn 10.34).[20]

Therefore, do not let this thought, or rather the evil one, trouble you, that bodily foods prevent you from attaining to those promises. No; for they are holy, and evil cannot issue from good, but only from those things that come from the mouth. The things that come from the heart (Mt 15.18–19) are the ones that prevent and hinder a person from arriving swiftly at the promises that lie before us. Therefore, when you submit to your physical requirements, do not hesitate at all, but do whatever your inner man can do to labor and humble its thoughts. Then, God will open the eyes of your heart in order to

---

[20]Although Barsanuphius and John do not adopt terms such as *theoria* or *theologia*, they do silently imply the notion of *theosis* in their correspondence.

see "the true light" (Jn 1.9) and to understand the words: "I am saved through grace" (Eph 2.5) in Christ Jesus our Lord. Amen.

The humility of Barsanuphius

125. Since the Great Old Man would meet with no one, except with his own attendant, the Abbot (Seridos), the same brother[21] entreated him in a letter to be deemed worthy of seeing him, saying that Abba Moses[22] and the other fathers would meet with those who asked. Therefore, the Old Man responded in a letter and with a prophecy, whose outcome we came to know through experience. For he told him that he would appear to him, revealing also the way and the reason for this appearance: "on account of the unbelievers in Judea" (Rom 15.31). After some time, when the same brother fell into the temptation of disbelief and said that there was no one in the cell of the Old Man, but the Abbot only simulated his presence, the Old Man invited this brother and others who were there, and washed the feet of them all. I, too, the sinner, was worthy of being washed. Consequently, the brother became sober and, recalling this response, confessed to us the same disbelief, as well as the Old Man's prophecy. And we all gave glory to God.

Now, the response of Barsanuphius is as follows.

Brother, no one "knows what is truly human, except the human spirit that is within" (1 Cor 2.11). Each person knows what is inside one's home and what is contained in one's purse. And, accordingly, one spends also for the nourishment of others. Moreover, we have a command from the Master not to build a tower unless we first consider the expense (cf. Lk 14.28).

[21]A monk, named Theodore. This and the following letter are addressed to the same Theodore.
[22]*Sayings*, Arsenius 38.

You have considered me among the saints, who are wealthy in spirit, and you have given me gladness with your knowledge, and indeed especially with your deeds. I am searching out their lives, and I am finding that their excess in good deeds corresponds to the excess of my evil deeds. They would indeed accept to meet with others, taking boldness in their actions; whereas, I do not accept to meet with others, and still tremble knowing my actions and fearing the one who says: "You, then, that teach others, will you not teach yourself?" (Rom 2.21) I am struggling to listen to the one who reproaches me and says: "Hypocrite, first take the log out of your own eye" (Mt 7.5), and so forth. I am laboring to take out this log but am unable to. However, I do not despair and I hope to achieve this.

Tell me the truth, brother; if someone should tell a pauper: "Certain people gave a generous donation; you, too, should give the same," could the pauper do this? Or is the pauper prevented by his own poverty? What else can I say? That those who are really thirsty and discover a source of refreshing water, are not curious about the source of the well itself, whether it comes from rainwater or river water. Others who are truly enjoying the brightness of the sun will not question whether it is near or far, whether it is material or not. The same applies to the other elements too. What about the fact that, when questioned on the subject of God, the fathers responded: "Seek the Lord, but do not seek where he dwells."[23]

What about you now? You abandoned your necessary task, which is dealing with your sins, and have sought to see me, who am an odorous worm, nothing but "earth and ashes" (Gen 18.27 and Job 42.6). Nevertheless, I too am foolish, and so I gladly sent you a response, being deceived and thinking that I am something, neglecting the words: "If those who are nothing think they are something, they are deceiving themselves" (Gal 6.3). Yes, certainly, I was deceived in this and spoke unworthily. Nevertheless, you should work like a good and obedient worker, no longer requesting this from me. For

[23] *Sayings*, Sisoes 40.

I too wish to see you, to embrace you and everyone else with the love that is according to God. At the right time, with God's assurance, I shall personally hurry to embrace everyone's feet, for the sake of receiving their intercession and prayer in order to be delivered "from the disbelievers in Judea" (Rom 15.31).

Let us not waste our little time in distractions, brother, but let us acquire mourning filled with tears, so that we may be blessed with those who mourn. Let us visit the poor and the meek, so that we may become their co-heirs. Let us seek peace with all, so that we may be found to be with the children of God. Let us endure insult and scorn, so that our reward may be increased in heaven (cf. Mt 5.3–12). And let us strive to reach his sight through good deeds, "so that people may see our good deeds and glorify our Father who is in heaven" (Mt 5.16). To him be the glory. Amen.

Brother, I am not writing these things to you in order to correct you; for I regard myself as a debtor with so many penalties. Rather, I fall down before the loving-kind God with unceasing supplications, that he might grant both to me and to you the forgiveness of sins, through the prayers of the saints. Amen.

Separation from one's spouse

129. *Question* from the same brother[24] to the Other Old Man. What, then, should I do? For my sorrow at being separated from my wife is persisting violently.

Response by John

It is written about man and woman: "The two shall be one flesh" (Gen 2.24). Therefore, just as if you were to cut off a member of your own flesh, the rest of the body would also be in pain for a while, until the wound is healed and the pain subsists; so also is it necessary for

[24]A monk, named Theodore.

you to be in pain for a while, since your very own flesh has been cut away.

The need for personal experience

154. *Question* from the same brother[25] to the Great Old Man. Please teach me how to reach abstinence and how to distinguish between natural weakness and demonic weakness. Moreover, how much should I eat?

Response by Barsanuphius

Brother, you are scraping little by little in order to reveal things that are hidden. Yet, being a fool, I think that no one except one who has reached this measure can distinguish what you ask me. For a living human being has a perception of warmth and coldness from those things that are brought to him. However, a dead person has no such perception; for a dead person has lost every perception. Likewise, one who learns comes to the measure of the science of letters, and is able to distinguish between them; but one who has neither learned nor is learning will be unable to grasp their meaning, even if such a person asks and is told tens of thousands of times. The same applies here as well. No matter how much you ask someone, one needs to have the experience itself.

As for your illness, if your body can accept daily food and is still slack, then this comes from the demons; otherwise, it is from the illness itself. Abstinence means getting up from the table with a little less (in terms of hunger and thirst), as the Elders ordained for their disciples.[26] When a person reaches the measure of the Apostle, who says: "For we are not ignorant of his devices" (2 Cor 2.11), then one

[25]An anonymous hermit.
[26]See Abba Isaiah, *Ascetic Treatise IV*. See J. Chryssavgis and P.R. Penkett, *Abba Isaiah of Scetis: The Ascetic Discourses* (Kalamazoo, MI: Cistercian Publications, 2002).

cannot fail to know how much to eat; for that person is trained. I am obliged, then, to speak about matters that are beyond me; however, there is no need for this. Perhaps those who are able to accept and understand these things are only few and rare. The God of our fathers will lead you to this joy. For this is an ineffable light, which is both brilliant and sweet. It does not remember bodily food and "forgets to eat its bread" (Ps 101.5). Its intellect is elsewhere, it seeks and meditates the things above, where Christ is seated at the right hand of the Father (Col 3.1–2). To him be the glory to the ages. Amen.

The rule differs from person to person

160. *Question* from the same brother[27] to the Other Old Man. Should everyone have the same rule that you told me, or do the elders respond according to the condition of the person asking?

Response by John

Brother, what I told your love about abstinence, I spoke to people like us and according to my own measure. So, if we can achieve the intermediate stage, we will progressively arrive at the greater measures. We should not wish at once to set our foot on the highest rung of all before we have placed it on the first rung of the ladder. For all those who come to the measure of which the Apostle spoke are able "to be full and hungry at the same time" (Phil 4.12), and so on; "for they are initiated in all things" (Phil 4.12). Therefore, you know your measures, brother. When temptation comes, I told you to cut down another ounce and, likewise, to drink less.

[27]Again, an anonymous hermit.

Approaching Holy Communion

170. *Question* from the same brother to the Other Old Man. If a fantasy occurs to me by night and, on the next day, there is Holy Communion, what should I do?

Response by John

Let us approach with all our wounds and not with any contempt, as people who are needful of a doctor, and he who healed the woman with the issue of blood (Mt 9.22) will also heal us. Let us love much, that he may also say to us: "Your many sins are forgiven; for you have loved much" (Lk 7.47). When you are about to take Communion, say: "Master, do not allow these holy things to be unto my condemnation but unto purification of soul and body and spirit." Then, you may approach with fear, and our Master, who is loving-kind, will work his mercy with us. Amen.

The power of love

187. The same person[28] suspected that the death of the Great Old Man was impending and grieved for his own salvation and that of the entire monastic community. So, he made this known to the same Old Man.

Most desired brother, you were moved according to God's love and have spoken words of humility, drawing to compassion even the unmerciful ones toward someone who is sinful and the least of all. What do I have to say to you, when I am a person with no compassion or mercy? I am constrained by your words, but have nothing to give you. If I had anything, I would have the following to say to you: "I shall not leave you now as orphans, during these years or at this

[28]A brother in the community of Seridos.

time. Behold, I remain with you by the command of God, who does all things for the benefit of us, his servants, and for the salvation of our souls." Nonetheless, even if this were to happen, it would not be for my own sake but for you that have asked this.

However, I am glad, although I am nothing, that you shall bear fruit to God while we still have time with one another. In this way, I shall be deemed worthy to lead you to my God, who always loves the salvation of us all, saying: "Here am I and my children, whom you have given me" (Is 8.18 and Heb 2.13), "keep them in your name" (Jn 17.11), protect them with your right hand. "Lead them into the harbor of your will" (Ps 106.30), "inscribe their names in your book" (Rev 21.27), and grant to them the pledge of life. I would tell them in order to make them rejoice: "Do not be afraid, little flock; for, it is your Father's good pleasure to give you the kingdom" (Lk 12.32).

Pray also that he might grant me to say: "Father, I desire that those also, whom you have given me, may be with me" (Jn 17.24) in the life that is ineffable. Believe me, brother, that the spirit is eager to say to my Master, who rejoices at the requests of his servants: "Master, either bring me with my children into your kingdom or else wipe me from your book" (Ex 32.32). However, my weakness and negligence prevent me from having such boldness. Yet, his mercy is great.

Therefore, since we have such a Master, let us take comfort, believing that he shall certainly work his mercy with us. God will not overlook the labor, the ascetic discipline, the mourning and the constraint of our fathers, both those who have fallen asleep and those who are now living. Instead, he will say: "I shall spare this place for my own sake and for the sake of those who have served and still serve me genuinely." I certainly believe without hesitation that there are some people here, in this very place, that are able to entreat God for the myriads of people; and these are not rejected. For he fulfills their will. They shall ask that the Lord's eyes may look upon this place day and night (1 Kg 8.29). For, indeed, already prayers have been sent to him for their sake, flashing as lightning and rising upward like the sun's rays, wherein the Father is gladdened, the Son rejoices, and the Holy Spirit exults.

Let us, then, only pay attention to ourselves, brother; for God is taking care of this place. In fact, it has become the resting-place of his servants, in whom is fulfilled: "There are glad songs of victory in the tents of the righteous" (Ps 117.15). So, it is up to the right hand of the Lord to exercise power, to give us strength, to grant us to follow in the steps of our fathers—their teaching, conduct, steadfastness, love, patience, persecutions, and suffering (2 Tim 3.10–11), and whatever else happened to them as a result of the enemy, things both pertaining to the senses and to the spirit.

For unless we possess something of their life, then how can we be their children? The Lord says: "If you were children of Abraham, then you would do the works of Abraham" (Jn 8.39). Unless we suffer with them according to the capacity of our weakness, then how shall we be glorified with them in that hour? Unless we die with them by cutting off our own will, even if a little, then how shall we be raised with them in the right hand portion, expecting to hear with great joy and gladness that blessed voice: "Come, you that are blessed by my Father, inherit the kingdom prepared for you from the foundation of the world" (Mt 25.34), and so on?

Brother, if God has granted our requests in order that we might have our fathers leading us and in order that we might be with them inseparably, both here and there, then let us be careful that we are not separated from them by our laziness, our slackness, our indolence, or our faithlessness. For it is said: "If the unbelieving partner separates, then let it be so" (1 Cor 7.15). Let us remember him who said: "The one who endures to the end will be saved" (Mt 10.22).

Let us pray to the Lord day and night in order that we may not be separated from our holy fathers either in this age or in the age to come. Where would we go? What more could we find? Where else might we be received? Let us not leave the light and seek the darkness; let us not leave the sweetness of honey and accept the bitterness of the serpent. Let us not be envious of one another and love

death; let us not hate life, let us not receive curses instead of blessings, let us not anger Christ or serve the enemy. Let us become vigilant, alert, swift, prepared. Let us awaken from our deep sleep; let us
understand what God has bestowed upon us in order that we should
be under the feet of his holy servants. Why do I even say "under the
feet"? We are actually their children and fellow heirs.

Blessed is the soul that has tasted these things! Blessed is the soul
that is illumined in order to understand them! Blessed is the soul
that has been wounded with such love! Blessed is the soul that is
taken captive by such things! Blessed is the soul that meditates on
them! Blessed is the soul that cleaves unto these things! Blessed is the
soul that has been counted worthy of them! Blessed is the soul that
believes in these things! Blessed is the soul that has been perfected in
them! For the joy, gladness, and reward of the kingdom are awaiting
such a soul, in the eternal light, before the angels and archangels and
all the heavenly powers, to the glory of the blessed Son, to the glory
of the blessed Holy Spirit. Amen. Brother, fare well.

Cleave to the Spirit

196. The same person[29] entreated the same Great Old Man to pray
for him and to declare to him how one is deemed worthy of the pure
and spiritual life.

Response by Barsanuphius

Beloved brother in the Lord, God has given us to walk easily in the
way of his will, which leads to eternal life. Let me tell you what this
is and how we are able to achieve this in order thus to acquire all of
the eternal goods. Since our Lord Jesus Christ has said: "Ask and you
shall receive; seek and you shall find, knock and it shall be opened

---

[29]A brother in the community of Seridos.

for you" (Mt 7.7), then pray to this good God in order that he might send his Holy Spirit, the Comforter, to us. When this comes, it shall teach us about everything (Jn 14.26) and reveal all of the mysteries to us. Seek to be guided by this Spirit. It will not allow deceit or distraction in the heart. It will not permit despondency or melancholy in the mind. It illumines the eyes, supports the heart, and uplifts the intellect.

Cleave to this, trust it, and love it. For it renders the foolish wise and bestows, teaches and grants strength and modesty, joy and righteousness, long-suffering and meekness, love and peace. Therefore, you possess a sure rock. Do not be negligent; for, the winds, rains and rivers are unable to prevail over the structure that is built upon it (Mt 7.24–25). You have the great helmsman, who rebukes the winds and the sea, and these are calmed, so that the ship is protected from sinking (Mt 8.26). You have the good teacher, who legislates that we should forget what lies behind and press on to the things that lie ahead (Phil 3.13).

Behold an inviolable treasure; behold an impregnable tower. Therefore, why do you reckon me as someone? Even I cannot come to these things unless I conquer wrath and stifle anger in order to acquire a condition of calmness, wherein the divine rests. Therefore, let us leave behind craftiness and assume integrity. Let us cultivate deep in order to plant a fruitful vine in our field, so that we may reap grapes and create wine of gladness, and so that we may become drunk and forget the afflictions and pains that control us unto the destruction of our soul.

Brother, it is the will of our Master that we may be saved. Why is it that we do not want this? Always then, pray fervently that the joy of the Spirit may come to us. For, when the fathers were filled with this Spirit, they cleaved unto it in perfect love, crying: "Who will separate us from the love of God?" (Rom 8.35) Furthermore, they replied: "Nothing." Therefore, let us love in order that we may be loved. Let us approach with all our heart in order that we may be received. Let us be greatly humbled in order that he might exalt us

(Mt 23.12). Let us weep in order that we may laugh (Lk 6.21). Let us be sorrowful in order that we may rejoice. Let us mourn in order that we may be comforted (Mt 5.5). Let us beseech that the Holy Spirit may come to us and guide us in the whole truth (Jn 16.13). For he does not lie, who says: "Seek and you shall receive" (Jn 16.24).

May the Lord accompany us in all things according to his mercy, in order that we may learn who we are, what we need, and what we want. To him be the glory to the ages. Amen.

Cleave to Jesus

199. Request from the same brother[30] to the same Great Old Man for prayer in order that he may abandon "the old self."

Response by Barsanuphius

Listen, beloved brother, and dedicate your heart to keeping the sacred words spoken to you not from mortals but from the Holy Spirit. Jesus is the physician of souls and bodies. If you have a wound, I shall lead you toward him and pray to him to heal you in both, that is if you also desire this. Our Lord, the Son of God, is the giver of all good gifts; and I am asking him to grant you not only your requests but exceedingly more than you request or imagine; and he tells me: "If he too desires this, then I shall grant it." Jesus is the Son of God, the light, and the strength, who was incarnate of the holy virgin Mary. "He was also seen on this earth and dwelt among people" (Bar 3.8), offering himself as "a living sacrifice, pleasing to God" (Rom 12.1) the Father for our sake, in order that he might prepare us "for himself as a chosen people, zealous for good deeds" (Titus 2.14), "a royal priesthood and holy nation" (1 Pet 2.9).

He who endured these things for our sake also left for us an example of patience; and he rejoices when we ask him. I am asking

30A brother in the community of Seridos.

him to illumine your heart in order to understand how he desires to make you prudent as well, through my nothingness. I am asking for you to receive strength; you, too, should request this. I am asking for you to be a son of God; you, too, should labor with me and sweat. For the Son of God says: "Come to me, all you that are weary and are carrying heavy burdens, and I will give you rest" (Mt 11.28).

Therefore, I approach him for your sake with much shame; however, unless you also approach, the shame is greater. I am also bearing his yoke and burden for your sake. Indeed, how you will hear this at the proper time! Jesus rejects no one. In fact, he even hired laborers for his vineyard at the eleventh hour (Mt 20.6). Cleave to him and make a little effort in order that you may receive the full reward equally like all the rest, as I too pray that you may. The Son of God became human for your sake; you, too, should become god through him. For he wants this, especially when you also want it.

Moreover, I pray that you may be liberated from the old man. However, you are found in this place. Therefore, if you struggle, the Son of God has given you an intellect; give him this in return unto heaven, "by seeking the things that are above and setting your mind on the things that are above" (Col 3.1–2), where he is found, "at the right hand of God" (Col 3.1), where I claim that you may reach, together with all those "who love his name" (Ps 68.37). For in this way one is liberated from the old self. Jesus said to the apostles: "You are the salt of the earth" (Mt 5.13). The earth is your body; for it is said: "You are earth, and you shall return to earth" (Gen 3.19). Therefore, become as salt unto yourself, salting and drying up the festering wounds and worms, namely the evil thoughts. If you do this, I too shall labor and salt with you, in order that they may not stench and disgust one another. God our savior wants us to be saved.

However, it is up to us to cry out without ceasing: "Save me, Lord, and I shall be saved" (Jer 17.14). For some people have cried out: "Behold, I have entered the harbor of your will" (Ps 106.30), into which I hope that you too will enter, if you give me a hand as best you can. Understand what has been said and adhere to it, and you shall attain, according to him who says: "Run, therefore, that you may obtain" (1 Cor 9.24). Pray for me, brother, so that I may not be condemned for speaking but not acting.

The role of the spiritual guide

203. *Question* from the same person[31] to the same Great Old Man about the progress of the soul, about advising a brother, and about faith in the same spiritual father.

Response by Barsanuphius

Believe me, much-desired one, that, with the grace of God, you are not standing outside the gates of the heavenly kingdom. However, stand well and pay attention to yourself with precision so as not to be cast out from there. For it is God's role to lead a person inside, through the prayers of the saints; and it is that person's role either to remain therein or to be cast out from there. And I am leading you progressively, with the will of God, to great heights. So take courage in the Lord and walk eagerly on his way, and you will receive assistance from him according to his will.

As for the brother, receive him with humble heart and tell him whatever God posits in your heart to say, bearing in mind that, when it was necessary, he even opened the mouth of the ass (cf. Num 22.28). And if everything depends on him, then attribute the benefit of everything to him, even the benefit that your brother receives through you. And if God sees your humility, he will attribute to you the reward of the advice, since you gave this word through your mouth. And then, what is written will be fulfilled in both of you: "A brother helping a brother is like a city fortified with ramparts" (Prov 18.19). May the Lord Jesus work with you to bring about all good.

[31]A brother in the community of Seridos.

As for me, the least servant, if God granted you his faith, then he is the one who increases and preserves it. It is not possible for him to reveal great mysteries to great people through the least of persons. For, he becomes "all in all" (1 Cor 15.28). Forgive me, father, and pray for me.

Do whatever you do for the sake of God

205. *Question* from the same brother[32] to the Other Old Man: I entreat you, venerable father, to condescend to my weakness and allow me, should one of the fathers wish to come to my cell in order to pray for me, to receive him. For I have witnessed myself burdened by despondency, until God establishes my soul through your prayers.

Response by John

I beg of your love, my brother, do not regard me as being superior than I am; for I am foolish and become boastful. And I must know that I am much inferior. For telling me that I must condescend signifies that I am sitting higher, at some great height. Do you not know that it is demanded of me that I should be below every person? For the one who is below everyone else has no place at all to which to descend.

You know the advice of the holy Apostle who says: "Testing all things, retain that which is good" (1 Thess 5.21). Everything that a person does out of godly fear is of benefit to the soul. Therefore, if the company of others is of benefit to you, it is not up to me to prevent you from such company. Otherwise, in so doing, I am also harming what is beneficial to you. So then, it is not only that I will not prevent you, but I even regard myself as being the most miserable of all those who come to pray for you in order to benefit you.

[32]A brother in the community of Seridos.

Therefore, whether or not you are in the company of others, may the Lord strengthen your genuine love in Christ. For why do I count myself among people, except in order that I may demand this of myself as well? Your gain is my joy.

What I think, therefore, is the following. Being in the company of others for the sake of God is a good thing; and not being in the company of others for the sake of God is also a good thing. When you are in the company, then, of those holy people who come to you for the sake of your benefit, ask them to pray for me that I may not be put to shame. This way you also will be doing the same thing for me, for the sake of love.

Constructing the house of silence

208. *Question*, once again, from the same person[33] to the same Great Old Man, asking whether he is permitted to practice silence.

Response by Barsanuphius

I have already spoken to your love, beloved brother, about silence, telling you that you should wait until now; not because I do not want you to reach the state of such a measure. Certainly not! However, I wish and pray that the Lord will grant you this state, and even more. For my joy is great whenever all of you show progress. Yet, these are spiritual gifts, given by God in their proper time, and it is he who calls and supports and protects. Indeed, it is said: "It is not those who commend themselves that are approved, but those whom the Lord commends" (2 Cor 10.18).

Therefore, if you wish to construct your home, first prepare the material and all other necessary things. And then, it is up to the professional builder to come and build the house.[34] The necessary

[33]A brother in the community of Seridos.
[34]Cf. Dorotheus, *Teaching 14*, 149–152. Silence is often compared to the

building materials for such a construction include firm faith for the building of walls, luminous wooden windows that allow in the light of the sun to brighten the house, so that there may be no darkness inside. These wooden windows are the five senses, affirmed in the precious Cross of Christ, which allow in the light of the spiritual sun of righteousness (cf. Mal 4.2), and do not permit any darkness to appear inside the house; and I am referring to the darkness of the enemy, the one who hates good.

Furthermore, you need the house to be covered by a roof, "so that the sun does not burn you by day, nor the moon by night" (Ps 120.6). The roof is symbolical of love for God, "which never fails" (1 Cor 13.8), which covers the house and does not allow the sun to set upon our anger (cf. Eph 4.26), so that we may not find the sun accusing us on the day of judgment, consuming us in the fire of Gehenna, nor again the moon bearing witness to our slackness and laziness by night, consuming us to eternal hell. Furthermore, the house needs a door, which allows the person dwelling there to enter inside and to be protected. When I speak of a door, brother, you should understand the spiritual door, namely the Son of God, who says: "I am the door" (Jn 10.9).

Now, if you prepare your house in this way, so that you do not have any of those things which are hated by it, he will come with the blessed Father and the Holy Spirit, and will make a dwelling in you (cf. Jn 14.23), teaching you what silence is and enlightening your heart with ineffable joy.

Receiving the Eucharist

212. *Question* from the same person[35] to the Other Old Man: When I give to my body more than is necessary, it does not help me during

---

construction of a house by the Patristic tradition: See Origen of Alexandria, the Desert Fathers, Evagrius of Pontus, and others.

[35]A monk, who was also a priest, in the community of Seridos.

the Liturgy; and if I give it less, I am afraid it will collapse completely. What should I do about this? And in regard to Holy Communion, since I want to partake of this every day, is it a burden to me that I approach Holy Communion as a sinner or should I continue to partake of it? And, again, how can I protect my life in silence?

Response by John

I have previously mentioned to your love, Abba, the words of John to the Savior; and yet you have written once again to me, the foolish and ignorant one. Therefore, if John[36] had then refused to respond, what can I who am disdained now respond? So I am speaking the truth when I say that I am nothing and that I know nothing. Yet for the sake of obedience, I speak that which I have in my heart. However, I will not say that it is exactly like this, but I am speaking according to what I am. God does not demand from the one who is ill any physical function, but only a spiritual function, namely prayer. For it is said: "Pray without ceasing" (1 Thess 5.17).

As for bodily diet, if the body cannot perform the Liturgy when it receives sufficient food, and if you are afraid of illness when it receives insufficient food, then keep to the middle way. Give it neither too much nor too little. Then the Scripture is fulfilled, which says: "Deviate neither to the right nor to the left" (Num 20.17). But give the body just a little less than it requires. For this is the way of the fathers: neither to be wasteful nor to be crushed in one's discipline. As for approaching Holy Communion, when this happens to you not out of ignorance but because of illness, then there is no condemnation. For the greatest physician goes himself to those who suffer greatly and are ill, just as our Lord Jesus himself came to us sinful and sick people. Forgive me, father, but I the unworthy one have spoken out of obedience.

---

[36]That is, the forerunner and Baptist John.

Forgiveness and struggle

240. *Question* from the same person[37] to the same Great Old Man:
Forgive me, Abba sir, for the sake of the Lord, because your holiness
said: "Behold, your faults are forgiven." Abba Isaiah also says that, so
long as a person retains the pleasure of these sins, they have not yet
been forgiven. Behold, I still retain their pleasure. For the sake of the
Lord, then, clarify these things for me. My thought is afflicted saying
that, since I am such a person, I should not have accepted ordination, since this too implies a sense of vainglory and responsibility. So
now I hesitate in my ministry as a deacon. At the same time, I
beseech you to answer me because my thought tells me that I have
been abandoned by God inasmuch as I have been weighed down
tremendously this last week by fornication.

Response

Oh the counsel of the evil demons! Oh the deceit of their leader, the
devil who hates good and hates people from beginning to end! For
just as he was separated from God, he desires that all people may per-
ish. Brother, I told you that your former sins have been forgiven, but
not that the warfare against them has also disappeared. A person
stands upright in contest. Even if you had no sins, the devil would
bring you their pleasure; and because you did have them, he does the
same, bringing you their pleasure. However, the way in which Abba
Isaiah spoke refers to the pleasures and to those who cultivate them.
For, indeed, it is one thing for someone to remember the sweetness
of honey, and another to have the taste as well as its memory.

So then, it is for the person who remembers the pleasure of sins
but who does not enact these pleasures—instead contradicting and
opposing them—that former sins are forgiven. Nevertheless, such
are the machinations of our enemy and adversary who always

[37] A brother, who was a deacon in the community of Seridos.

desires to devour all people (cf. Ps 123.3), in order to lead to despair, in regard to salvation, and to hopelessness, in regard to life, all those who are not established on the firm rock (cf. Mt 7.24; Lk 6.48) of faith, according to which measure everyone will receive their reward (cf. Prov 24.12; Mt 16.27). Therefore, guard yourself against these in order that you may not fall entirely into the hands of the devil; and the Lord who lives to the ages will have mercy on you.

As for your ordination, who dares to call himself worthy except one who is truly mad and completely ignorant? Therefore, condemn yourself and at the same time minister to God in the lot that has been given you; for to him belong the mercy, support, and strength. During the Liturgy, remember the words: "Serve the Lord in fear, and rejoice in him with trembling" (Ps 2.11), as well as the words: "He makes his angels spirits and his ministers a flame of fire" (Ps 103.4). Do not be afraid; God has not abandoned you. For if we do not abandon him, he does not abandon us. It is his will that we return to him and be saved (cf. 1 Tim 2.4).

As for you being weighed down tremendously by fornication, this happens by having thoughts against and judging your neighbor. It also happens from speaking boldly with those I told you not to. If those who want to become wealthy in the world often take risks on journeys by sea and land, and endure these risks, how much more so should we who eagerly await the kingdom of heaven in order to be proclaimed children of God (cf. Mt 5.9). We hear that "our contest is not against flesh and blood, but against principalities and against powers" (cf. Eph 6.12).

Until now, you have not struggled against sin to the point of blood. Does the spirit of listlessness, then, already paralyze you? What have you endured? What have you borne? What variety of temptations have you endured rejoicing? Ah sleepy monk! Show the devil that you live for God, taking refuge in him, moving hands and feet, swimming in the onslaught of the spiritual waves which rise to the heavens and drop to the abyss (cf. Ps 106. 26). God is my witness, that my heart has been unfolded with you, as the God who fashioned it knows, he who set it in the covenant of the sacred commandments within, in order to lead you out—with the power of God—from darkness to true light and from the death of condemnation to the life of righteousness. Pay attention to yourself, brother, for it is impossible to be saved without labor and humility.

On serving at the altar

241. *Question* from the same person[38] to the same Great Old Man: Father, since your holiness ordered me to serve at liturgy, declare to me, I beseech you, what I should ponder or meditate as I stand before the altar with the priest, or when I am cutting up the holy bread or offering people to drink of the Holy Blood, or again when I am carrying Communion and taking it to someone. And should I have a special vestment for liturgical use or a covering for my legs?

Response by Barsanuphius

Brother, all of this is a spiritual allegory, and you understand it literally. The deacon serves like the Cherubim, and ought to be all eye, all intellect,[39] with his intellect and thought looking upward, with fear, trembling, and doxology. For he bears the Body and Blood of the immortal King. He even assumes the face of the Seraphim in proclaiming the doxology and in fanning the hidden mysteries as with their holy wings, recalling through these wings their levitation from this earth and from things material, crying out ceaselessly with his intellect in the temple of the inner man (cf. Rom 7.22) the victory hymn of the magnificent glory (cf. 2 Pet 1.17) of our God: "Holy, holy, holy, Lord God of Sabaoth; heaven and earth are full of your glory" (Is 6.3). And from the dreadful and fearful voice of this proclamation, the devil falls away, trembling from the captive soul,

[38]A brother, who was a deacon in the community of Seridos.
[39]Cf. *Sayings*, Bessarion 11.

and the demons are made to flee in confusion and shame, leaving it free from their slavery.

So now the soul sees that the true light (cf. Jn 1.9) has dawned upon it; and directing its attention, it sees the beauty of the immortal lamb and seeks to be filled with his Body and Blood. Then it hears the loud voice of David crying out and saying: "Taste and see that the Lord is gracious" (Ps 33.9). And approaching with fear, it becomes a partaker of his Body and Blood, and this taste becomes indelible in the soul, protecting it from every passion.

"Meditate on these things" (cf. 1 Tim 4.15) whether you are standing before the holy mysteries, or else dividing or distributing the drink, or when carrying Communion to someone or gathering up the holies, and simply in every service that you perform at the altar. As for your vestment, acquire a spiritual cloak in which God is well pleased. The covering for your legs signifies the mortification of the members (cf. Col 3.5). Tell me, brother, if a person wears a purple, fully silken robe and yet is a fornicator, does the clothing purify that person from fornication or from the other passions? What then shall they do who are worthy of the holy mysteries but who lack garments? The Lord ordered us to have one garment (cf. Mt 10.10), and that is the garment of virtues, of which may God make us worthy to the ages. Amen.

Remembrance of death

242. *Question* by the same person[40] to the same Great Old Man: Master, forgive me, and pray for me for the sake of the Lord, that my senses may be sanctified. In fact, your holiness said that the deacon ought to be like the Cherubim and the Seraphim; yet I am polluted in the senses. What shall I do that my ministry as a deacon may not be to my condemnation? For, I am wretched and cannot control

[40]A brother, who was a deacon in the community of Seridos.

myself. For God's sake, help me so that I may not lose my soul in every way.

Response

Do your best always to have this memory of how the deacon ought to be and of how you actually are, remembering death and how you are going to encounter God. And in continually condemning yourself, your heart feels compunction in order to receive repentance. For, he who said by the prophet: "Be first to confess your sins, so that you may be justified" (Is 43.26 LXX), this same one justifies you and renders you innocent of every condemnation. Indeed, it says: "It is God who justifies; who is it then that will condemn you?" (Rom 8.33).

So, as I have on other occasions stated to you, acquire humility, obedience, and submission, and you shall be saved. And do not argue at all, saying: "Why this, and why that?" but become obedient, especially to your Abbot who after God cares for you and has been entrusted with your soul. And if you have the zeal to keep these things, I shall do abundantly more than I possibly can, so that God may grant you the strength to make this possible. The Lord shall keep you and protect you from the evil one. Amen.

Advice to a deacon

244. Another brother, who was a deacon, excused himself from serving in the altar, recalling his past sins. So he asked the same Great Old Man about this, as well as about his bodily sickness.

He responded in the following way.

Brother, Scripture has taught us that "those who desire to lead a pious life according to Christ will be persecuted" (2 Tim 3.12). Yet how is it possible to be persecuted even in the present age? It is from the demons, which persecute them out of fear of God and his worship. However, "repentance from sin is no longer committing this sin,"[41] while abstaining from evils is riddance of these. Do not let the former grieve you, and do not be hindered from serving as a deacon before God but do so with fear and trembling (cf. Phil 2.12); and pay attention to the fact that it sanctifies your soul. And if you believe this, you will always tremble in order not to sin, so that you do not lose this sanctification. Therefore, endure passions and afflictions thankfully, for they are a discipline from God, and he will have mercy on you, and they shall be for the salvation of your soul. Amen.

If you fall, rise up

268. *Question* from the same brother[42] to the same Great Old Man: Holy father, I beseech you to ask for me to receive strength from God because whatever I determine for myself when I am alone, I lose it when I come to be with other brothers. And I am afraid that I am become accustomed only to sinning and repenting, but not to correcting myself. In this way, I shall stay with my sins until my death. For, I know that the afflictions of the passions are beneficial to me inasmuch as they crush the hardness of my soul. And let me not, the fool that I am, wish to be relieved of these from now. However, father, what I am asking through your prayers, is whether it is beneficial for me not to be conquered continually in order that this may not afflict my heart.

Response

No one ever says to another: I am bearing your concern, and then stays without concern; for, in this way, that person is found to be an

---

[41] *Sayings*, Poemen 120.
[42] *Letters* 268 to 330 are addressed to Dorotheus of Gaza. See *introduction*, above, section iv.

impostor. However, the brother whose burden is being held must also contribute some small effort and do his best with vigilance in order to keep the commandments of his fathers. And if he should fall once, then he should rise up again. And I trust in God that, even if he is caught out once and strives again to rise up, then he will not become accustomed at all, nor will he be negligent. But God will quickly bring him to the order of the zealous ones and will not take his soul until he leads him to a noble measure, to the degree of maturity.

So do not relax, but while you yet have time before you, work, be humble, obey, submit, and God will be at your side. For he grants grace to the humble and resists the proud (cf. Prov 3.34). Say continually: "Jesus, help me;" and he shall help you. May God liberate your soul from the passions of dishonor, child.

The spiritual fire of desire

277. *Question* from the same brother to the Other Old Man: Which is the way to salvation? Is it through labor, or through humility? And tell me about forgetfulness.

Response by John

True labor, brother, does not come without humility. For labor of itself is in vain. It is said: "Consider my humility and my labor, and forgive all of my sins" (Ps 24.18). One who has these will reach salvation quickly. And one who has humility with disregard of oneself has reached the same point, because disregard of oneself is equivalent to labor. Now, someone who has humility itself alone, will certainly enter, but more slowly. And if someone wants to possess genuine humility, that person should not reckon himself as being anything; for, this is true humility.

One who receives the fire, which the Lord came to bring into the world (cf. Lk 12.49), does not know forgetfulness and captivity, since that person always has a perception of the fire. Take an example from material fire. If a person is breathing his last and fire approaches, that person will immediately feel pain. In fact, no matter where a person is held captive, if a burning coal falls on him, then that person will not stay there even for a moment. Fire, brother, is not quenched; otherwise, it is not fire. Therefore, if you want to be rid of forgetfulness and captivity, there is no other way to do this unless you acquire for yourself the spiritual fire. For its warmth consumes those things. And one acquires this fire through desire for God.

Brother, unless your heart labors in everything in search for the Lord, you cannot progress. If you spend time on these matters, you will arrive at them. For it is said: "Be still" (Ps 45.11), and so on. May the Lord grant you to understand these things and labor in them.

True humility

278. *Question* from the same brother to the same Old Man: Father, what is humility? And what is disregard of oneself? What is contrition of heart? And does one acquire humility by disregarding oneself in the heart? Or is it necessary also to have external injury and insolence from people? And must someone who feels humble also speak humbly and look to achieve humble things?

Response

Humility means not reckoning oneself as anything in every situation and cutting off one's proper will in everything and calmly enduring whatever occurs on the outside. This is true humility, in which there is no room for vainglory. The person who feels humble does not need to seek to speak humbly, but it is enough for that person to say: "Forgive me and pray for me." Nor is it necessary for that person to seek after humble matters of oneself. For both of the above create vainglory and do not allow one to progress. Nevertheless, when one receives an order and does not contradict this, then one is certainly led to progress.

There are two kinds of disregard of oneself: one is from within the heart, and the other from injuries received from the outside. The second is greater, namely the one that comes from the outside. For the one that comes from the heart requires less labor than the one that comes from other people, because the latter creates more pain in the heart. Guarding one's own heart is contrition of heart.

True modesty

279. *Question* from the same person to the same Old Man: If a person receives praise from someone, should that person respond in a modest way?

Response

Silence is of even greater benefit. For if one responds, it is as if one accepts the praise; and this is vainglory. The same goes for the response, which seems to that person to be modest; this too is vainglory. For one is saying about oneself whatever one so feels. Indeed, if one were to hear the same thing from someone else, one would not be able to bear it.

Silence before praise

280. *Question* from the same brother to the same Old Man: However, it sometimes happens that the other person thinks that, by keeping silent, one is accepting the praise, and so that person is scandalized. What, then, should one do?

Response by John

In regard to things unseen, the struggling monk should allow God to reassure the listener. For how does that person know whether the other has not been edified rather by his silence, by not accepting the praise, instead of being scandalized? If the other person reveals the opposite, then one ought with humility to inform that person saying: "Forgive me, brother, for I recognize no good in myself, and this is why I found nothing to say in response to you. Nevertheless, for the Lord's sake, pray for me."

False praise

281. *Question* from the same brother to the same Old Man: It sometimes happens that someone who is indeed a sinner will speak the truth in humility and not in vainglory. Should this person also not respond in a similar circumstance?

Response by John

This person, too, should not respond. For even if this person is for a while speaking in humility, yet the one listening may regard that person as being humble and so the former will again bear the burden. The Lord said: "Woe to you, when people speak well of you" (Lk 6.26). He is referring to sinners, who are praised but do not have corresponding deeds to show.

Humble realism

282. *Question* from the same person to the same Old Man: So how is it that we find some of the guileless fathers responding in modesty when they are praised?

Response

The fathers reached that measure of which the Lord spoke: "When you have done all these things, say 'we are worthless slaves'" (Lk 17.10). And in truth, since they consider themselves in this way, they respond according to what they are. Moreover, even if someone else accuses them of being worthless slaves, they are not annoyed, but they even bless that person as speaking the truth.

The primacy of silence

283. *Question* from the same brother to the same Old Man: If one receives an act of kindness from another person and expresses exceeding gratitude by enumerating the kindnesses, should the benefactor again not respond in this case?

Response

Silence is good in every case. Nevertheless, in order not to appear as if rejecting the thanks, the benefactor should say with humility: "Forgive me, abba, and for the Lord's sake pray for me," believing in his heart that he did not do anything. For it is the Lord who is the benefactor of us all. And one should also pray to God not to be judged even for these words.

The godly criterion

287. *Question* from the same brother to the same Old Man: If I feel that some matter is beneficial for certain brothers, should I tell them even if I am not asked to speak? In addition, if one of these happens to be my superior or a priest, should I mention it to the Abbot or should I keep silent? And then, if I am asked, what should I say? And

if it is indeed beneficial for me to speak of my own accord, how should I speak? For I wish to honor my monastic habit and speak neither with supposed humility nor with the authority of a teacher. For God's sake, forgive me.

Response

The fathers said that: "One who speaks for God is doing a good thing; and one who is silent for God is also doing a good thing."[43] This saying of the fathers may be interpreted in the following way. As I have told you, one who speaks without passion is doing a good thing; for that person is speaking for God. And one who sees that one is about to speak with passion and therefore keeps silent, is also doing a good thing. For, that person is keeping silent for God.

If you are about to say something according to God, do not be concerned about what you will say, because then you are abolishing the commandment (cf. Mt 10.19). Rather, cast the matter before God, and he will grant to your mouth what it is that you should say for the benefit of all. God knows how to gird us weak ones with strength, and he will strengthen you, brother.

On speaking with humility

290. *Question* from the same person one to the same Old Man: Since you have declared to me that I should speak with humility, if I am asked about something or happen to see something, what does it mean when you say that I should do it "with humility"? And if I notice my heart taking pleasure in the vainglory of speaking, or if I do not take pleasure at that time but foresee that this will come upon me later, should I be silent or not?

[43] *Sayings*, Poemen 147.

Response

Saying something with humility means not speaking as a teacher, but as one who has heard from the Abbot or the fathers. If it is beneficial to speak to your brother and the vainglory of pleasure tempts you, then pay attention to yourself because it may wish to prevent you from benefiting your brother; and if you listen to this vainglory, your brother will never benefit from you. Instead, reprimand this vainglory and despise it; and after speaking, repent to God, saying: "Forgive me, for I have spoken in vainglory." The same applies to your second question.

Do whatever comes naturally

302. *Question* from the same person to the same Old Man. Since I perceive that, when I make a prostration before certain people, I blush a little out of vainglory, should I avoid making such prostrations before those people, or should I simply do whatever comes naturally?

Response by John

Do not deliberately seek to make prostrations before certain people or privately; simply do whatever comes naturally.

Dealing with passions

304. *Question* from the same brother to the same Old Man. If a passionate thought enters my heart, in what way should I reject it? By contradicting it? By rebuking it, in order to become angry against it? Or by hastening toward God and casting my weakness before him?

Response by John

Brother, the passions are afflictions. And the Lord did not distinguish between them, but rather said: "Invoke me in the day of your affliction, and I shall deliver you, and you shall glorify me" (Ps 49.15). Therefore, in the case of every passion, there is nothing more beneficial than to invoke the name of God.

Contradicting a passion does not belong to everyone, but only to those who are strong according to God, who are able to subdue the demons (Lk 10.20). For if someone who is not strong contradicts them, then the demons will ridicule that person for being inferior to them and yet contradicting them. Similarly, rebuking the passions belongs to the great and powerful ones. Whom among the saints will you find rebuking the devil like St Michael (Jude 9–10)? Indeed, he had the power to do so.

Those of us who are weak can only take refuge in the name of Jesus. For according to Scripture, the passions are the demons, and they are to be cast out (Acts 8.7 and 16.18). What more do you want? God will strengthen you and empower you in his fear.

Journeying on the middle way

314. *Question* from the same person to the same Old Man. My thought tells me that silence is more necessary and more beneficial to me than anything else. Is it this correct?

Response by John

Silence is nothing else than restraining one's heart from giving and taking (Phil 4.14), from people-pleasing and other such actions. When the Lord rebuked the Scribe by telling him about the man who fell among thieves, asking him who was his neighbor, the Scribe replied: "The one who showed mercy on him" (Lk 10.37). Again, he said: "I desire mercy and not sacrifice" (Mt 9.13). Therefore, if you have heard once that mercy is greater than sacrifice, incline your heart toward mercy.

For the excuse of silence brings one to arrogance before one even gains oneself, namely before one has become blameless. Indeed, that is when one reaches silence, when one bears the Cross. Therefore, if you are compassionate to someone, you will find assistance; if you restrain yourself, supposedly to transcend these limits, then you should know that you will lose even what you have. So do not move to one or the other extreme; but journey on the middle way, knowing what is the will of God "because the days are evil" (Eph 5.16).

Silence and service

315. *Question* from the same brother to the same Old Man. Master, make it clear to me how I can avoid the two extremes in order to journey in the middle way. Should not certain days be explicitly set aside for silence and other days for service?

Response by John

Neither bold in one's silence nor despising one's silence in times of distraction: such is the middle way, where one is prevented from falling by having humility in silence and vigilance in distraction, as well as by restraining one's thought. There is no limit to the hours of silence; how much more so is this the case with the days of silence. Rather, one should bear everything that comes one's way with thanksgiving. Moreover, one should suffer with all those in the monastic community, thereby fulfilling the commandment of the Apostle, namely that if one is afflicted, one should share in the affliction (1 Cor 12.26) in order to comfort and console that person. That is what compassion is.

It is a good thing to suffer with those who are ill and to contribute to their healing. For if a doctor receives a reward in caring for the sick, how much more so will someone who suffers as much as one can with one's neighbor in all things? Indeed, unless one is compassionate in all things, then even that in which one is compassionate will reveal one's proper will.

Medicine and spirituality

327. *Question* from the same person to the Great Old Man. Since you have tested me and found me capable of this service in the hospital, declare to me, father, whether I should read some medical books and practice them on my own or rather be carefree of and avoid these things as distracting the intellect and as giving rise to vainglory for my soul, since I am not vigilant. I could be content with the knowledge that I have and offer healing with oil, fire, ointments, and other such simple things as are used by those who do not read medical books. What, then, should I do? For my heart trembles before this ministry, fearing that I might make mistakes, thereby adding more sins to my passions.

Response by the Great Old Man

Since we have not yet reached perfection, in order to be entirely rid of the captivity of the passions, it is beneficial for us to dwell on medical matters rather than the passions. However, we should not place our trust in these, but only in the God who grants death and life, who says: "I shall strike, and I shall heal" (Deut 32.39). When you read these books and ask others about these matters, do not forget that without God there can be no healing.

One who applies oneself to medicine should do so in the name of God, and God will help him. The art of medicine does not prevent one from practicing piety; you should regard the practice of medicine as the brothers' manual labor. Do whatever you do with fear of God and you will be protected through the prayers of the saints. Amen.

Pay attention to yourself

330. *Question* from the same brother to the same Great Old Man. Merciful father, I fall down before you again and shall not cease to disturb you until you strengthen me. For whenever God grants me a little sorrow for my sins through your prayers, I gradually lose it through my outward distraction. Therefore, I ask you to secure this for me as well, so that everything may be from God's mercy or from you and nothing from me. I can do nothing at all on my own, unless I am strengthened through your holy prayers. As far as the administration of the hospital, father, I am afraid that the authority might contribute to my vainglory and boldness. It is natural for me to be burdened by gluttony when I continually handle food matter. So, perhaps you should test me with some humbler charge; then, I shall make some progress and be relieved a little before once again being charged with serving others. You know, father, that I am not declaring these things because I have despaired in the charge assigned to me. For what can I do, the wretched one? I am afraid, father, that by staying here in my cell I am exciting my passions, whether of my own or from the demons, I think. I do not know; but reveal to me the will of God, father, and lift me out of the thoughts that trouble me, strengthening me through your prayers, in order to do what you say; and forgive me.

Response by Barsanuphius

Brother, listen and be assured in the Lord that, since the time that we permitted you to assume this charge, our hand and our heart are with you. Rather, the hand of God is with you; for we entreat God through prayer for the salvation of your soul and your strengthening in this charge in order that it might prosper and be protected. There is no other way for you to be saved than this. Therefore, do not become despondent. When you fall, arise; when you err, blame yourself until the Lord shows you the mercy you desire. Simply do not be neglectful. Take courage in the fact that the Lord who established you in this work will also direct it. We, too, bear your concern with you.

Therefore, do not let the devil deceive you with any pretense to rights. "By smooth talk and flattery they deceive the hearts of the simple-minded" (Rom 16.18). The one who assigned you to this charge is the same one who said to his disciples: "Behold, I am sending you out" (Mt 10.16); and again: "Behold, I am with you" (Mt 28.20). Do not be afraid and do not concern yourself with anything of the hospital, growing despondent about the concern of authority. You only need to pay attention to yourself as much as you can, and God will come to your assistance. Fare well in the Lord, taking strength in him.

Regard your neighbor as yourself

339. Another brother[44] asked the Other Old Man. It is a commandment of the Lord that we love our neighbor as ourselves (Lev 19.19 and Lk 10.27) and that we be joyful and sorrowful with him as if he were our own member (1 Cor 12.26). Therefore, to see our neighbor in poverty and ignore him is a transgression of love, even if we only have what we need and are unable to cover his needs. Tell me, then, father, how is love revealed in this case?

Response by John

Love toward one's neighbor is manifested in many ways and not only in giving something. Listen to some other ways. If you travel

---

[44]A monk in the community of Seridos.

somewhere with your neighbor and find that your thought wants to be honored more than he, rather than rejoicing that he is honored in the same way as you, in this respect you do not regard him as yourself. For the Apostle said: "Outdo one another in showing honor" (Rom 12.10). If you have something to eat and notice your thought wanting to eat alone on account of desire and not of need, in this respect you do not regard him as yourself. Even if you only have enough for whatever you need, if you do not give him some of this, in this respect you do not regard him as yourself. Indeed, if we wish to apply the Scriptural word in this way, it will not be able to stand. In fact, this was not written for one person alone, but every person is called our neighbor (Lk 10.36–37). Therefore, how can you fulfill this commandment in all people when you do not have enough to give everyone?

Again, loving one's neighbor as oneself is also like this: If some loss occurs and you notice your thought taking pleasure in the fact that he is harmed more than you, then again in this respect also you do not regard him as yourself. Or if you see him praised and do not rejoice with him, believing that you too have been praised with him; if you did not actually say that your brother's praise also extends to you—for, he is your member—then you have not tried to regard him as yourself. The same applies in so many other cases. Furthermore, regarding one's neighbor as oneself means that if you have heard from the fathers about the way of God and your brother asks you, then you should not withhold his care and benefit for the sake of envy. Rather, knowing that he is your brother, you should tell him whatever you heard according to godly fear, without regarding yourself as a teacher; for, this does not benefit you.

Command and counsel

369. *Question* from the same person.[45] Father, you showed me the difference between a command and godly counsel. Give me also the

[45]Another brother in the community of Seridos.

signs of each: how are they recognized and what is the power of each?

Response by John

If you approach a spiritual father in order to ask about something not so much because you wish to receive a command but only to hear a godly response, and you are told what you should do, then you should still keep this word by all means. If, in doing so, you are tempted by affliction as a result of this, do not be troubled; for this is happening for your benefit. Now, if you do not want to do what you have been told, you should not think that you have transgressed a command. For, you did not receive it as a command; however, it seems that you have been overlooking what is beneficial for you and so you should blame yourself for this.

Indeed, you should consider everything that comes out of the mouth of the saints as being for the benefit of those who hear them. The same applies, even if you did not ask anything, but the elder's thought was inspired by God to speak to you of his own accord, something which actually happened once. For one of the elders once sought to visit a city. Another elder said to him of his own accord: "If you visit the city, you shall fall into fornication." He disobeyed, visited the city, and fell into this sin.

If you ask about a specific matter wanting to receive a command, then you should make a prostration and ask for a command to be given to you. When the command is received, you should again make a prostration, so that the one who gave you the command may bless you, saying: "Bless me, father, as I receive the command; and pray that I might keep it." Learn this, too, brother, that the command is not given without reason, and so the one who gave the command will assist you in supplication and prayers, in order that you might be able to keep it. Now, if you are distracted and do not make a prostration in order to receive a blessing, do not think that the command is given without reason. For it holds even if you received it without cause or consequence. So, if you can, labor in this, and do not hesitate to go and make your prostration in order to receive the blessing. If, however, you are unable to do so, then consider that you have received the command with negligence.

On false knowledge

373. A brother[46] asked the excellent Old Man: What is false knowledge?

Response by John

False knowledge is trusting in one's own thought, that things are as they appear to us. Whosoever wishes to be delivered of this should not trust in one's own thought, but ask one's elder. If the elder responds and his response is what the brother thought, then one should still not trust in one's own thought, saying: "I was ridiculed by the demons in order to be persuaded by my thought that I have true knowledge, so that once I have believed this, they might lead me in other ways to fall on my head. The elder spoke the truth because he speaks from God. He is not at all ridiculed by the demons."

I have said what I could to my brother; in the final analysis, however, I do not know if this is so. Pray for me.

On giving thanks worthily

404. *Question* from the same brother:[47] How is it possible to give thanks to God worthily?

---

[46]Another brother in the community of Seridos.
[47]A pious layman. *Letters* 404 to 483 are addressed to various laypersons in the vicinity and brothers in the community.

Response by Barsanuphius

People who are nothing forgive one another for the slightest thing, and even relieve them from terrible afflictions, so that they profess their gratitude and proclaim to everyone the good that was received. How much more so, then, should we give thanks, who receive benefits from God in every way! With what words can we thank him, who before all else created us, then offered us assistance against our enemies by giving us prudence of heart, health of body, light in our eyes, breath of life, and, above all, a place of repentance and the possibility to receive his Body and Blood for the forgiveness of sins and the establishment of our heart. For, it is written: "Bread to strengthen the human heart" (Ps 103.15). And if anyone thinks that this refers to material bread, then how is it that the Spirit again says: "One does not live by bread alone, but by every word that comes from the mouth of God" (Deut 8.3)?

Now, if people give rewards and thanks for material and corruptible things, what can we ever return to the one that was crucified for us, if we too wish to be grateful? We should endure everything for him until death. Do not, then, toil in your effort to understand the gratitude that people, and especially sinners, owe to God; after all, he died for them. If someone goes to prison for you, you will want to thank that person exceedingly. How much more so for the one who dies for you? Learn this; we never come to the point of thanking God worthily. Nevertheless, let us thank him as much as we can, with our mouth and heart, and he is so loving-kind toward us that he will count and number us with the copper coins of that widow (cf. Mk 12.42).

Enough, however, for the sinners who want to give thanks; because the righteous give more than thanks, even when they are cut up and put to death, according to St Paul, who says: "Give thanks" (1 Thess 5.18), obviously to God. To him be the glory to the ages. Amen.

On good and evil

405. *Question* from the same brother to the same Old Man: Is it possible for the demons to do good to anyone? And how is it revealed that this comes from the demons? And what is the difference between this and a divine gift?

Response by Barsanuphius

There is a possibility, theoretically, that good can come to someone from the evil one with the purpose of deceit. However, every good that comes from the devil in order to deceive us, when examined closely, is found to be disguise. For he is a liar, and you cannot find truth in him, as the final result will display. For the final result of his light is darkness, according to the Apostle who says about the angels of the devil, that they can be disguised into ministers of righteousness: "Their end will match their deeds" (2 Cor 11.14–15); and according to the Savior who says: "You will know them by their fruits" (Mt 7.16).

So if you examine with knowledge and discernment, you will certainly find that in the supposed good that comes from the devil, there is no trace of good but only vainglory or turmoil or something else similar. Whereas God's good always abounds in illumination and humility of heart and brings us to calmness. Now, if unknowingly we suffer some harm from the deceit of the evil one, and later learn about this temptation, let us come to ourselves and take refuge in the one who alone can abolish this temptation. It is also necessary to know that the saints immediately and easily perceive the difference, whereas sinners only perceive it at the end. Just like when an experienced goldsmith receives gold, he is able to say what it is even before putting it through fire; whereas, an inexperienced person will know only after putting it through fire.

Discerning good from evil

406. *Question*. Once the supposed good of the demons is exposed, explain to me how one can escape the danger that comes from it?

Response by Barsanuphius

We are always obliged to regard the good as being good. However, if the good is tested in the act and found to be evil, it is necessary to reject it in the same way as someone who finds something to drink and thinks that it is good, but on tasting it finds it to be bitter. Then, immediately, one spits it from one's mouth, even while one's mouth becomes numb through the bitterness. The same happens with chestnuts, almonds, and the like. Of course, that person is not to blame for the taste. However, if the same person learns about its bitterness and persists in consuming it, filling his stomach with the bitterness, then one can only blame oneself.

The same also applies here. Therefore, if a person is deceived but afterward learns and says: "I have been deceived, Lord Master, forgive me," God will forgive that person, for he is merciful. Learn this, too, beloved one; God does not allow us to be tempted beyond our capacity (cf. 1 Cor 10.13). So in all things, let us offer supplication to him, and he will distinguish for us the good from the supposed good. To him be the glory to the ages. Amen.

On dreams

418. *Question*. I have heard that if a dream appears three times, then it is true. Father, is this so?

Response by Barsanuphius

This is not true. Nor should you believe in any such dream. For the one who appears to us once in the form of a lie, can also do the same three times and many times. Therefore, do not be ridiculed, brother, but pay attention to yourself.

Unceasing prayer

425. *Question.* When it seems that the thought is calm and not being afflicted, is it not a good thing at that time to refrain from invoking the name of the Master Christ? For the thought suggests to me that since we are now calm, there is no need for it.

Response by Barsanuphius

We should not have such peace, if we consider ourselves as being sinners. For it is said: "There is no peace for the wicked, says the Lord" (Is 48.22). If, then, there is no peace for the wicked, then what sort of peace are you experiencing? We should be afraid, because it has been written: "When they speak of peace and security, then all of a sudden destruction comes upon them, as labor pains come upon a pregnant woman, and there will be no escape" (1 Thess 5.3).

There are also times when the enemy craftily makes the heart find a little rest, in order that it may not invoke the name of God. For, the demons are not ignorant of the fact that they are annoyed by the invocation of God's name. Therefore, knowing this, let us not cease invoking the name of God for our assistance; for, this is the best prayer. It is also said: "Pray unceasingly" (1 Thess 5.17), and unceasingly implies without end or limit.

On thoughts during prayer

427. *Question.* If, while I am reciting the Psalms or praying or reading, an inappropriate thought arises, should I pay attention to it and interrupt my psalmody or prayer or reading in order to oppose it with appropriate thoughts?

Response by Barsanuphius

Show contempt to yourself and pay close attention to your psalmody and prayer and reading in order that you may be able to receive strength from the words that are recited. For if we accept to spend time with the thoughts of the enemy, then we would never be able to do anything good, which is precisely what the enemy is looking for. And when you notice that you are so congested by such thoughts, that they are bothering you in your psalmody or prayer or reading, even then do not struggle against them; for this is not something within your control. Rather, strive to invoke the name of God, and he will come to your assistance and abolish the machinations of the enemies. For his is the power and the glory to the ages. Amen.

On compunction during prayer

428. How can one acquire compunction in prayer and reading and psalmody?

Response by Barsanuphius

Compunction comes to a person from continuity of remembrance. Therefore, when one is praying, one must prayerfully bring one's actions to memory, recalling how those who do these things are judged, and hearing the fearful voice: "Depart from me, you accursed ones, to the eternal fire" (Mt 25.41), and so on. When I speak of remembrance of sins, I do not mean the recollection of specific individual sins, in case the adversary intrudes again and brings us into some other form of captivity. I simply mean the remembrance of the fact that, as sinners, we are debtors. And if the hardness remains even after all this, then do not surrender; for often this tolerance occurs to us from God for our testing, to see if we will endure.

As far as reading and psalmody go, one must keep one's intellect alert to the words of the text and assume within one's soul the power that is concealed in them. If the words are about good deeds, then we should strive to perform good deeds; if they are about the punishment of evil deeds, then we should strive to avoid the expected threat of those who do evil. And by persisting in such recollections, do not surrender if the hardness also happens to insist. For God is merciful and long-suffering, and he awaits our ascetic struggle. Always remember the Psalmist who says: "I waited patiently for the Lord, and he inclined to me" (Ps 39.1), and so on. As you spend time on these matters, hope that the mercies of God will come upon you quickly.

The power of the word

429. *Question.* When I try to pay close attention to the meaning of the words of the Psalmist, it often happens that they cause me evil thoughts.

Response by Barsanuphius

If you see that the enemy has craftily used the very words of the Psalms to bring warfare upon you, it is not necessary to stay too closely attached to the meaning of the words, but simply recite these with vigilance and without distraction. For even if you are merely repeating the words, the enemies know their meaning and will not be able to resist you. Then, your psalmody will become not simply a supplication to God, but also an abolition of the enemies.

Remembering God's name

430. *Question.* If I am reciting the Psalms or else happen to be with other people, and my thought afflicts me, if I say the name of God in my heart, since I cannot do so with my mouth, or even if I simply remember his name, is this perhaps not enough to receive divine assistance?

Response by Barsanuphius

If you are standing in the choir while it is chanting the Psalms, or if you happen to be with other people, and the thought comes to you to say the name of God, do not suppose that, because you are not saying it with your mouth, you are not in fact naming God. Remember that he knows people's hearts and pays attention to your heart. So, go ahead and say his name in your heart. For this is what is said in Scripture: "Shut your door and pray to your Father who is in secret" (Mt 6.6). This means that we are to shut our mouth and pray to him within the heart. Therefore, one who shuts one's mouth and says God's name, or else prays to him in one's heart, is fulfilling this Scripture. Even if you do not mention his name in your heart, but simply remember him therein—for this is still more powerful than saying the name—it is still sufficient for you to receive divine assistance.

Meditation and prayer

431. *Question.* So is it good for someone to meditate or pray constantly in the heart, even if the tongue does not fully cooperate? When this happens to me, my thought is deeply plunged and I feel burdened, so that I imagine I am seeing things or fantasies, and I even live in my dreams.

Response by Barsanuphius

This belongs to the perfect, who are able to direct the intellect and keep it in the fear of God, so that it may not deviate and be plunged to the deepest distraction or imagination. However, one who is unable always to maintain vigilance according to God grasps a hold of oneself and connects the meditation to the tongue as well.

For the same occurs with those who swim in the sea. Some are experienced swimmers and confidently throw themselves into the water, knowing that the sea cannot sink those who have good skills in swimming. Yet, someone who is still a novice in these skills, who feels the waters causing him to sink and is afraid of drowning, removes oneself from the ocean to the shore. And after regaining one's breath a little, the same person will again lower oneself into the deep water and continue to make an effort to acquire the skills of swimming completely, until one reaches the level of those who have previously mastered them.

On dealing with thoughts

432. *Question.* What does it mean when one of the fathers says that it is not for the thoughts which enter our intellect that we are judged, but for handling them badly? Abba Joseph said to one of the brothers: "Cut off your thoughts quickly"; while to another brother, he said: "Let them enter, and exchange conversation with them, so that you may be tested."[48]

Response by Barsanuphius

When the thoughts enter our intellect, it is like the seed being sown, and this is not to our condemnation. However, when we consent to these thoughts, that is when we are handling them badly, and this is certainly to our condemnation. As for the difference between allowing the thoughts to enter and cutting them off, it is as follows. One who is capable of resisting and waging warfare against and not being defeated by these thoughts, allows them to enter; one who is weak and unable to do so, possibly even giving consent to them, should cut them off in order to flee toward God.

[48]Cf. *Sayings*, Joseph of Panephysis 3.

On using the left hand

437. *Question.* If I perform the sign of the Cross with my left hand, because I am unable to do so with my right hand, is this improper?

Response by Barsanuphius

Well, as for me, whenever I want to perform the sign of the Cross over my right hand, I certainly have to use my left hand to do so.

A time to speak . . .

442. *Question.* My thought tells me that I am sinning in everything that I do, and that I must say with every word, deed, and thought: "I have sinned." For if I am not continually confessing my sin, I may consider myself as being without sin. And I am greatly grieved with both thoughts. For it is not possible for me to say this every time; but if I fail to do so, I feel that I have not sinned.

Response by Barsanuphius

We should always be assured that we are in all things sinful, alike in deed and in word and in thought. However, to say every time: "I have sinned" is not possible. In fact, it is an act of the demons, who want to throw us into despondency. Likewise, we should not feel confident to say, each time, that we have not sinned. Instead, let us remember the words of Ecclesiastes: "There is a time to speak and a time to keep silent" (Eccl 3.7). And in the morning for the night, as in the evening for the day, let us say with compunction in prayer to our Master God: "Master, forgive me everything for the sake of your holy name, and heal my soul; for, I have sinned before you." And this will be sufficient for you. Just as someone who has an agent, from whom one receives various amounts of money, cannot keep full account each time, but simply takes it for granted. The same occurs in this case.

Distraction in prayer

443. *Question.* When I recite the Psalms, my mind wanders or is distracted. What should I do?

Response by Barsanuphius

If you are distracted, then take up the same Psalm from the last word that you remember. And if this happens once, or twice, or three times, and you cannot remember which point or find any word that you remember in the part you have just recited, then take up the Psalm from the very beginning. If it happens that you have read through most of the Psalm, in order not to be further interrupted or fall into despondency, then recite from the following Psalm. For the aim of the enemy is to prevent us from giving glory through forgetfulness. So, then, starting from the following Psalm is doxology; but not being distracted belongs to those who have purified senses, while we are still weak. However, when we become conscious of the distraction, let us keep vigilant in order to understand the words from that point onward, so that they are not to our condemnation.

Prayer without distraction

444. *Question.* If I am distracted during prayer, what should I do?

Response by Barsanuphius

If you are praying to God and become distracted, struggle until you begin to pray without distraction. And keep your intellect alert in order that it does not become too lofty. Nonetheless, should this occur, since we are weak, persist to the very end of your prayer; then prick your heart, and say with compunction: "Lord, have mercy on me and forgive me all of my offenses." And, afterward, you will receive forgiveness of all your offenses as well as of the distraction that occurred at the beginning of your prayer.

The way of salvation

450. A brother asked the Great Old Man: Have mercy on me, and tell me how I might be saved. For, I have promised my thought to submit to the contents of your letter.

Response by Barsanuphius

If you truly want to be saved, listen to my words and put them into practice. Raise your feet from the ground[49] and lift your intellect up toward heaven; and let your meditation stay there day and night. And as much as you can, despise yourself, struggling to regard yourself as being beneath every other person. This is the true way. Outside of this, there is no other way for someone who wants to be saved in Christ, who gives us strength (cf. 1 Tim 1.12). Let the one who wants run! Let the one who wants run! Let the one who wants run! Let that person run in such a way as to win (cf. 1 Cor 9.24). I bear witness before the living God, who desires to grant eternal life to everyone who so wants. If you want, brother, apply yourself to this.

The essential way

451. *Question* from the same person to the Other Old Man: Why did the good elder say: "Let the one who wants run!" three times?

[49]That is, arise from your slothfulness.

Response by John

In order to demonstrate how useful this way is, and that there is no way more essential than this. This is why he repeated his words three times. For the Lord also did the same in the Gospel according to Matthew, when he repeated his words twice: "Amen, amen, I say to you" (Jn 1.51), because he was saying things that were more substantial at that time.

On not condemning our neighbor

453. *Question.* If I notice someone doing something inappropriate, should I not judge this as being inappropriate? And how can I avoid condemning this neighbor of mine?

Response by John

If this matter is truly inappropriate, then we cannot but condemn it as being inappropriate. Otherwise, how can we avoid the harm that comes from it, according to the voice of the Lord, who said: "Beware of false prophets, who come to you in sheep's clothing but inwardly are ravenous wolves; you will know them by their fruits" (Mt 7.15–16). However, the one who is actually doing the inappropriate deed should not be condemned, according to: "Do not judge, so that you are not judged" (Mt 7.1), but also because we should regard ourselves as being more sinful than all others.

Furthermore, we should not ascribe the sin to our brother but to the devil who deceived him. For just as when one pushes someone else towards a barrier, we would blame the person pushing, so it is also in this case. It may even be that someone will do something which appears inappropriate to those watching, but which is really done with a good intention.

This happened once to the holy Old Man.[50] For as he was walking

---

[50]That is, Barsanuphius.

past the hippodrome on one occasion, he entered inside, fully conscious of what he was doing. And when he saw each of the competitors striving to overtake and triumph over one other, he said to his thought: "Do you see how the followers of the devil eagerly race against each other? How much more so should we who are the heirs of the kingdom of heaven?" And, as a result of that spectacle, he left that place more eager in his spiritual journey and ascetic struggle.

So, again, we do not know whether through his repentance, the sinful brother will be more pleasing to God, like the Publican who in an instant was saved through humility and confession. For it was the Pharisee who left condemned by his own arrogance. Therefore, in consideration of these things, let us imitate the humility of the Publican and condemn ourselves in order to be justified; and let us avoid the arrogance of the Pharisee in order not to be condemned (cf. Lk 18.10–14).

We all require healing

463. A Christ-loving layperson asked the same Old Man if one should reflect a great deal about the sacred mysteries, and whether a sinful person approaching these would be condemned as being unworthy.

Response by John

When you enter the holies, pay attention and have no doubt that you are about to receive the Body and Blood of Christ; indeed, this is the truth. As for how this is the case, do not reflect on it too much. According to him who said: "Take, eat; for this is my body and blood" (Mt 26.26–28), these were given to us for the forgiveness of our sins. One who believes this, we hope, will not be condemned.

Therefore, do not prevent yourself from approaching by judging yourself as being a sinner. Believe, rather, that a sinner who approaches the Savior is rendered worthy of the forgiveness of sins, in the manner that we encounter in Scripture those who approach him and hear the divine voice: "Your many sins are forgiven" (Lk 7.47–48). Had that person been worthy of approaching him, he would not have had any sins. Yet, because he was a sinful man and a debtor, he received the forgiveness of his debts.

Again, listen to the words of the Lord: "I did not come to save the righteous, but sinners" (Mt 9.13). And again: "Those who are well have no need of a physician, but only those who are sick" (Lk 5.31). So regard yourself as being sinful and unwell, and approach him who alone can save the lost (cf. Lk 19.10).

Silence and conversation

470. *Question.* There are certain conversations that are indifferent, bearing neither sin nor profit. These may include conversations with someone about, say, the prosperity of cities or their turmoil or peace, or about wars that are going to break out, or other such matters. Is it inappropriate to speak about these matters as well?

Response by John

If silence is more necessary even during conversations about good matters, how much more so in matters that are indifferent? However, if we cannot keep silent, being overcome by conversing with others, let us at least not prolong the conversation in order not to fall into the snare of the enemy through chattering too much.

Tempted to speak

471. *Question.* Well, there are many occasions when I come to such chattering by discussing matters that are indifferent; and no one escapes sin by chattering. So what should I do?

Response by John

Let us maintain some measure for ourselves in this way. If we have noticed that we have been overcome by the thought to speak once, then let us try our best to prevent this from happening a second time. If we are overcome a second time, then let us be prepared to prevent it from happening a third time; and let us progress in this way during every conversation. So, if the number of occasions that we are given to speak is ten, and one is overcome by temptation nine times and prevents it on the tenth, then one is found to be better than the other who has been overcome by the temptation to speak ten times.

Conversation and company

472. *Question.* Now, if I find myself among people speaking about certain matters, whether fleshly or spiritual, what should I do? Should I speak or not?

Response by John

If you find yourself in the company of people conversing about either worldly or spiritual matters, give the impression that you too are contributing something, while saying nothing that harms the soul. Bear in mind that you should avoid their praises, lest you appear to them to be silent and are later burdened by this. However, even if you do this, make sure that you do not condemn them as speaking much, simply because you are saying little. For you do not know whether what will burden you will actually be the one word that you have spoken rather than the many words that they have spoken.

Discernment in conversation

475. *Question.* It happens that I am conversing with someone; and, after beginning the conversation, the evil one suggests turmoil. What should I do then? For if I delay the conversation in order to discern my words, to understand them the way that you have just said, whether they are good or evil, then I offend the person listening because all of a sudden I am silent.

Response by John

If it is not apparent to you that your words are sinful, then you should complete your sentence and discern afterward whether you have spoken evil things. Thus you can discipline your thought, condemning it as speaking evil in order that it may not say any more. For it is written: "Child, you have sinned; do this no more" (Sir 21.1). And thenceforth, you should pay attention before speaking, to determine whether the subject is beneficial for you to join in conversation; and only then should you begin to converse. For if it is clear that the subject is sinful, then even if there is no turmoil suggested by your thought, you should strive to remove yourself, either pretending that you had forgotten about it or transferring yourself to some other conversation that is more useful, in order not to fall into condemnation through this.

Conversation and silence

476. *Question.* Father, since you said that before even beginning the conversation it is necessary to examine the thought, what happens when necessity demands that I speak immediately? For example, when I am sitting in the company of others, in order not to appear to be silent to them, I too want to speak on the subject. After all, I cannot notice any obvious sin in the conversation, but in fact it

appears to me to be good, or at least indifferent. What do you order me to do, since I do not have the time to discern with precision whether there is any sin hidden therein?

Response by John

If the conversation appears good, or at least indifferent, and necessity demands that you speak, then say something. However, if you notice that your words will bring you vainglory, or that those listening will certainly praise you, then you should do everything possible in order for your thought not to accept this vainglory. Furthermore, if you see that you are overcome by it, then it is more beneficial for you to be silent rather than to be harmed.

Tension in relations

483. A brother happened to be working with another brother, and was struck by the latter at the instigation of the devil. Being troubled by this, he sought to be relieved of working with that brother. So he asked the Great Old Man about this.

And Barsanuphius responded in the following manner.

Brother, in regard to what you have asked me, do not be troubled or do anything with turmoil, especially against a person who is already troubled by his thoughts and by the envy of the devil. You too have been tempted and enraged by thoughts on other occasions. And if you recall how you also were tempted at that time, you will not scorn your brother in his own time of temptation. Many people who have been afflicted with some illness involving drowsiness of the head, which comes from extremely high fever, do not know what they are thinking or saying, even when they are insulting those who are well and perhaps even attending to them; for their illness has overcome them. The same applies now.

Even if one were to tell your brother about a doctor, he would not accept healing; nor does he know what is beneficial for him, but he receives anything that one tells him as utter craziness. Instead, he insults others and is furious, seeking foods that harm rather than heal; for he knows not what he does. That is what happens to a person who is tempted; even if that person's soul is being destroyed, that person is not aware of this. In fact, that person is unaware of even insulting and scorning the saints, who suffer with him for his own soul; for he is dizzy with the suffering of the illness.

At the same time, the adversary always turns things against him, until he forces him to deny God himself. That is exactly what is happening in this situation. However, God knows this, and providentially allows us to be tempted in order that we may appear to him as proven and in order that we may endure our neighbor in the time of his material and spiritual weakness. For it is said: "Bear one another's burdens, and in this way you will fulfill the law of Christ" (Gal 6.2).

Thus, for someone who lives with a sick person, this means that what is important is not doing that person's will or giving that person something that is harmful, but rather bearing that person's insults and other burdens, and attending to that person and taking care not to offer anything harmful. The same can be applied to this case. Your concern should not be to do the will of the one who is asking, but to pray for that person. And if that person is unable to do so himself, then he should ask those who can, to beseech the Master God in order to deliver him from the temptation that has befallen him. Then such a person becomes like Martha and Mary, the sisters of Lazarus, who asked the Master to resurrect their brother (cf. Jn 11.21 and 32). And if one does this, one should not feel superior; for this is happening to him through others, and he should be doing the same for others. "For the measure that you give will be the measure you get back" (Lk 6.38).

And do not think that, because your brother has struck you, you have suffered something great; for, the Lord of heaven and earth was also beaten, and suffered so much more. Do not be moved to exchange your place or be separated from your brother; for this is not according to God, but in fact the fulfillment of the devil's will. Even if you should do this, the temptation will not go away, but will come to be worse; for no good can come from evil. So this actually signifies lack of submission and lack of prudence. "For where there is envy and selfish ambition, there will also be disorder and wickedness of every kind" (Jas 3.16). No one is ever healed of these to the ages, except by cutting off one's own will and struggling not to interfere with one's neighbor or ever to say: "What is this?" or: "What is that?" And one who says: "I want that too" becomes the son of the devil and is estranged from God. It is clear that such a person wants to fulfill one's own will and not God's.

So take courage, brother, God will protect you! Pray with all your soul for your brother, and love him in Christ Jesus our Lord, to whom be the glory to the ages. Amen.

Temptations and thoughts

496. Supplication from the same person[51] to the same Great Old Man: Abba, have mercy on me, for the Lord's sake. For when I am resting alone, images arise within me, including a fear that people are assaulting me, to the point that I am afraid even when I am asleep; and so I cannot rest. In fact, since I am a coward by nature, the temptation swells up even more fiercely and does not allow me to sleep at all; of course, as I said, this is from my fear and little faith. This results also in bodily exhaustion, so that I can hardly even move. Master, you surely know what is beneficial for me. So, do me a favor and respond, good father. Forgive me, for I am a sinner and in a very bad state.

[51]A brother, who was formerly a soldier.

Response by Barsanuphius

Brother, you should give glory to God for demonstrating how Scripture is true. For it is said: "God is faithful, and he will not let you be tested beyond your strength" (1 Cor 10.13). Therefore, he allows you to be tested according to your strength; while those who are great, he tests according to their own strength with diverse temptations, and they rejoice in this. For temptation brings us to progress; and wherever there is good, there also temptation occurs. So do not be afraid of temptations, but rejoice that they are leading you to progress. Simply scorn them, and God will assist you and protect you.

Tensions in spiritual direction

504. *Question.*[52] If one happens to live with an elder who is unable to respond to questions, when the brother is in fact troubled by thoughts, should one ask another elder, whether with or without the knowledge of one's own elder? Or should one endure and be crushed by one's thoughts?

Response by Barsanuphius

If one knows that one's abba will benefit the soul, one should confide in him, saying: "I have thoughts; what do you think that I should do?" The elder, like someone who has an ill child and hurries to take it to a doctor—in fact, even spending all of his income to care for this child—will also gladly take his disciple to someone with the gift of healing, or else send him to find someone else. If one knows that the elder cannot endure this, then he should not say anything but simply look for an opportunity, when God will provide an occasion, to ask another spiritual elder about one's thoughts, entreating him

[52]From a brother monk.

not to inform his own elder because this would throw him into the passion of envy.

This of course will create great affliction inasmuch as one is asking another elder while not being scandalized in one's own elder for not possessing such a gift; for such a gift is not given to everyone. Nevertheless, if one searches carefully, one will discover that one's own elder has another gift. For the gifts of the Spirit are diverse and distributed variously among people (Rom 12.6), to one in such a manner while to another in a different manner. Now, if one does not find the opportunity to ask someone else, then one should endure, praying to God for assistance.

On medication and healing

508. *Response* by the same Great Old Man to the question from the same person[53] about whether he should take medication.

Brother, some people use doctors and others do not. Those who do, use them with hope in God, saying: "In the name of the Lord, we entrust ourselves to doctors; for he shall grant healing through them." Those who do not use doctors, do so with hope in his name and he heals them. Therefore, if you do use doctors, you are not doing something wrong; and if you do not use doctors, do not be arrogant. I say this because you need to remember that when you use doctors, it is the will of God that occurs and nothing else (Sir 38.1–15). However, if you wish to abide by the word of Elijah (1 Kg 18.15) in regard to thinking only about today,[54] then you will be carefree.

[53]A brother, who was ill. *Letters* 508 to 532 are addressed by Abba John to the same brother.
[54]*Life of Antony*, ch. 7, PG 26.853.

Physical exhaustion and prayer

519. *Question.* How is it that I feel extremely tired, especially when I rise to chant the Psalms at night, as if I were unwell? Whatever I do, I do as a burden. Is this perhaps physical weakness, or is it from the demons?

Response by John

The matter of physical weakness is quite clear. For, if the body cannot tolerate the regular food, it is evident that it is unwell and one should relax in one's ministry. However, if the body tolerates the customary food and does not rise for liturgy, it is evident that this comes from the demons. It is, then, necessary to force ourselves, always according to our strength and never beyond this. If the heart is vigilant (Song 5.2), then sleep is nothing for the body; this is like a person who is almost snoring and, when he hears robbers breaking in, does everything possible to escape them. Thus, if we are able to understand, we shall see that we are exactly like this.

Illness and passions

520. *Question.* Father, tell me whether an illness can come from God, and how one may recognize this.

Response by John

It can indeed. Therefore, when one perceives any illness and no troubling passion is present, then this illness comes from God and will dispel the warfare. It is necessary, in this case, to condescend a little to the body. When, however, an illness is present together with a passion, then we should not condescend at all. For, it is demonic, and condescension will only increase the passion.

Therefore, it is beneficial to discipline the body wherever warfare prevails, even if one succumbs to illness; nevertheless, one should not cast the soul into illness in order to support the body. On the other hand, if the illness or cause of indisposition is manifest, when for example the body is weakened by some journey, namely from the heat wave, then one should condescend—always moderately and never excessively—because the demons also mingle their own interests in this.

Medication and perfection

529. *Question.* Father, tell me whether those who are ill and yet despise medicine and food have reached the measure of perfection.

Response by John

Those who have despised medicine and food have reached the measure of faith (Rom 12.3) but not of perfection.

On diet and faith

530. *Question.* If, then, someone does not have this kind of faith, should that person examine which foods are beneficial for one's illness or merely avoid those foods, which are harmful? And if it happens that a certain food is neither harmful nor extremely beneficial, should one partake of this without fear?

Response by John

One should only avoid the harmful foods. If a certain food happens to be neither harmful nor beneficial, one should not eat to the point of satiation but only a little. For if one eats to the point of satiation, even from a food that is beneficial, one is harmed.

Spiritual and physical healing

532. *Question.* Since, as you have said, making use of a doctor in the name of God is not to be rejected,[55] although leaving everything up to God with faith and humility is even better, my thought tells me: "If some physical illness comes upon you, you should show a doctor; for being healed without medicine is beyond your measure." Then again, it tells me not to make use of these, but instead to use the holy water of the saints and be content with that alone. I entreat you, compassionate father, tell me which of these I should keep to.

Response by John

Brother, since I observe that you seem to care a great deal about the illnesses of the body, I should say that the fathers are not preoccupied with these. Your second thought, then, is better than the first. For, that thought has perfect faith in God, while the other reveals lack of faith. The second has patience, which brings one to testing (Rom 5.4), which gives rise to hope that does not shame; the other contains hesitation, the sister of pusillanimity, wherein dwells faithlessness, the mother of doubt, which estranges us from God and leads us to destruction.

One makes us friends of God; the other makes us his enemies. One introduces us to the kingdom of heaven; the other leads to Gehenna. One lifts the head (Ps 109.7) and grants boldness before our Master and God; the other bows the head in shame, and makes us stand before God without confidence. One glorifies us; the other dishonors us. One cuts off our captivity and makes us carefree in order to cast our every concern before the Lord (Ps 54.23 and 1 Pet 5.7); the other casts captivity and other evil occupations within our heart. One brings edification; the other leads to the slackening of those who consider it. One is filled with wisdom, namely with the

[55]See *Letter* 508.

understanding that someone who is able to heal the hidden passions will also be able to heal his own passion; the other is filled with foolishness in regard to God, wondering whether he can heal or not. One is characterized by a peaceful state and teaches the person that does not despair; the other is characterized by a troubled state. One makes people travel throughout cities and towns; the other is free from such things. One plants sorrow within the heart and consumes it; the other places thanksgiving, which intercedes well for the salvation of all people before the great doctor, who bears our illnesses (Is 53.4; Mt 8.17).

As for me, my genuine brother, although I am completely reluctant, I have never shown myself to a doctor; nor have I taken any medicine for my wounds. I have done this not out of virtue but out of reluctance, refusing to travel to cities and towns in order not to burden anyone or trouble anyone with helping my unworthiness, fearing the future defense at the expected hour in regard to whatever I have done. Whoever is able to endure this out of virtue is blessed; for such a person becomes a sharer in the patience of the holy Job.

I also remember that many women, too, courageously endured their physical illnesses, leaving everything to God. Indeed, I am embarrassed for even being called a man. Thus, the woman with the issue of blood renounced her former condition when she learned that worldly doctors were in no way able to help her, although she had spent all her living among them. Indeed, she assumed a different condition and hastened toward the great and spiritual heavenly doctor, who heals both soul and body, and the illness disappeared even before the decree was given (Mt 9.20–22). Moreover, the Canaanite woman renounced the secular people, the sorcerers, ventriloquists, and magicians, seeing that their art was both useless and demonic, and hastened to the Master saying: "Have mercy on me, Son of David" (Mt 15.22). Indeed, the fact of her healing by the loving-kind doctor was proclaimed to everyone from one end of the world to the other.

I am omitting the rest in order to concentrate on these, in order that I may someday reach their faith (Eph 4.13) and not fail to gain their beatitude. These two are sufficient for me as a rebuke of shame; so it is not necessary to introduce here the faith and humility of the centurion, who not only renounced the doctors and others in order to come to the Master, but even deemed himself unworthy to bring him into his house. He simply said with faith: "Only say the word, and my servant shall be healed" (Mt 8.8). His faith was great, and our Savior praised it.

In saying these things, I am condemning myself; for I do not desire enough, or strive, or fall down to the ground, or even know when the hour of my judgment will arrive, wretched as I am. When shall I be called? When will the fearful and severe angel come in order to lead away my wretched soul with reprimand? When will the door close, in order for me to stay and cry with the five virgins (Mt 25.10–11), while no one will hear me? It is clear that these things trouble me in the present moment; and it is no secret that slackness and reluctance have overcome me.

What, then? Should I despair for myself? Surely not! For such a sin is unto death (1 Jn 5.16). Nevertheless, I entreat you, brother, shed your tears upon me bitterly, as if over a dead person, who has long been stenching in the tomb. We know the results of tears; for the experience of Peter's mourning has taught us (Mt 26.75). Pray for me, who am saying these things but who do nothing good, that the good doctor may also be compassionate upon me and heal the illnesses of my soul and body. To him be the glory to the ages. Amen.

On silence and patience

554. The same brother[56] asked the Other Old Man. My thought tells me that if I want to be saved, I should leave the monastic

---

[56]A brother, who was a carpenter in the community of Seridos.

community and practice silence, as the fathers have said. For I am not benefiting in this art of carpentry, because it brings me much turmoil and affliction.

Response by John

Brother, it has already been declared to you that it is not beneficial for you to leave the monastic community. Now, then, I am telling you that if you do leave, you will end up falling. Therefore, you know what you are doing. If you truly want to be saved, acquire humility, obedience, and submission, namely the cutting off of one's proper will, and you shall live in heaven and on earth (Mt 6.10).

As for the silence, of which the fathers speak, you do not know what this is; indeed, not many people know. For this silence is not a matter of shutting one's mouth. There may be someone who speaks tens of thousands of words that are useful, and this is reckoned as silence; there may be another who speaks only one idle word, and this is reckoned as trampling the Savior's teachings.[57] For he said: "On the day of judgment you will have to give account for every careless word you utter" (Mt 12.36).

Since you also say that you do not benefit from the art of carpentry, believe me, brother, you do not know whether or not it is beneficial for you. These are tricks of the demons, who show your thought whatever they want in order that you may establish your own will and disobey that of your fathers. For whoever wants to know the truth asks the fathers whether one is benefiting or being harmed. And whatever they say, that person believes and practices that which is beneficial.

Many people have paid a price in order to be insulted and to learn patience. Yet, you are learning patience at no cost, since the Lord says: "By your patience you shall gain your souls" (Lk 21.19). We should give thanks to the person who afflicts us; for through him,

[57]See *Sayings*, Poemen 27.

we acquire patience. Do not let the devil tempt you. May the Lord assist you. Amen.

Criticism of others

561. *Question.*[58] If someone is not actually criticizing another person but is gladly listening to criticism, is he too condemned for this?

Response by John

Even listening gladly to criticism is criticism and receives the same condemnation.

Holiness and the salvation of the world

569. Supplication from the fathers living in silence within the monastic community to the Great Old Man in regard to the world. Since the world is in danger,[59] all of us entreat you, as your servants, to pray to God's goodness, so that he may lift his hand and return the sword in its sheath (1 Chr 21.27). Stand upright among those who have fallen and who live with your holy incense, and put an end to this destruction (Num 16.35). Raise the holy altar in the holy threshing-floor (2 Sam 24.18–24 and 1 Chr 21.15–26) of Arauna, in order that God's wrath may cease (Job 14.13). We entreat you; indeed, we beseech you, have compassion on the world that is perishing. Remember that all of us are your members (2 Sam 5.1; Eph 5.30). Display your compassion and God's wonders (Dan 4.2–3) even in the present time. For his is the glory to the ages. Amen.

[58]From a brother in the community of Seridos.
[59]This letter possibly refers to the plague that occurred in Palestine between 542–543 during the reign of the Emperor Justinian.

Response by Barsanuphius

Brothers, I am in mourning and desolation (2 Macc 11.6) in regard
to the impending wrath. Indeed, we are doing things contrary to the
will of God. For he said: "Unless your righteousness exceeds that of
the Scribes and Pharisees, you will never enter the kingdom of
heaven" (Mt 5.20). So, our transgressions have surpassed those of
other peoples. There are many people who entreat God's loving-
kindness to cease his wrath from the world; and, of course, none is
more loving-kind than God, who desires to have mercy and opposes
the multitude of sins that occur in the world.

There are three men, perfect in God, who have exceeded the
measure of humanity and received the authority to loose and bind,
to forgive and hold sins (Mt 18.18 and Jn 20.23). These men stand
before the shattered world (Ps 105.23), keeping the whole world from
complete and sudden annihilation. Through their prayers, God
combines his chastisement with his mercy. And it has been told to
them, that God's wrath will last a little longer. Therefore, pray with
them. For, the prayers of these three are joined at the entrance to the
spiritual altar of the Father of lights (Jas 1.17). They share in each
other's joy and gladness in heaven (Eph 1.3). And when they turn
once again toward the earth, they share in each other's mourning
and weeping for the evils that occur and attract his wrath. These
three are John in Rome and Elias in Corinth, and another in the
region of Jerusalem.[60] I believe that they will achieve his great mercy
(Ps 50.3). Yes, they will undoubtedly achieve it. Amen.

May my God strengthen you to hear and believe and bear these
things; for, they are unbelievable to those who do not understand
them.

---

[60]Nikodemus of Mount Athos believed that Barsanuphius was in fact the third
of these.

On doing evil unintentionally

611. *Question.*[61] Who are the ones that sin and do evil intentionally, and who are the ones who do so unintentionally?

Response by Barsanuphius

Those that do evil intentionally are the ones who surrender their will to evil, who take pleasure in and become acquainted with it. These people are at peace with Satan and do not war against him in their thoughts.

Those that do evil unintentionally are the ones who, according to the Apostle, have a power that opposes them in their members (cf. Rom 7.23). This is a misty power and veil. Yet in their thoughts, they neither consent, nor take pleasure in, nor again obey, but rather contradict, oppose, reply, counterattack, and are angry at themselves. These people are considered as being much more beautiful and precious in God's eyes than those who choose to surrender their will to evil and take pleasure in it.

On endurance in illness

613. Exhortation by the holy and Great Old Man, Barsanuphius, to a novice who was ill and could not bear the affliction of his illness.

Brother, those workers who demanded their reward from their master, had nothing else to be proud of but their claim: "We endured the burning heat and the toil of the day" (Mt 20.12). Therefore, let us endure affliction gladly in order that the mercy of God may richly come upon us. And let us not be discouraged and fall into despondency; for this brings us to the beginning of destruction. Son, remember: "The one who endures to the end will be saved" (Mt 10.22).

[61]From another brother in the community of Seridos.

Child, the illness is also there to tempt us, and the temptation is there to test us: "After all, one who is not tempted is not tested," since trial in danger proves a person, just like gold in fire (cf. Wis 3.6). For trial brings one to hope, and hope does not disappoint (cf. Rom 5.4–5). So do not break down; nor allow the enemy to paralyze your intention according to God and shake your faith in the Holy Trinity.

After all, what happened to you in order for you to break down? Tell me. Remember what the Apostle says: "In your struggle against sin you have not resisted to the point of shedding your blood. And you have forgotten the exhortation that addresses you as children: 'My child, do not regard lightly the discipline of the Lord, or lose heart when you are punished by him; for the Lord disciplines those whom he loves, and chastises every child whom he accepts.' Endure trials for the sake of discipline. God is treating you as children; for what child is there whom a parent does not discipline? If you do not have that discipline in which all children share, then you are illegitimate and not his children" (Heb 12.4–8). If you bear the affliction gratefully, then you have become a son. If you break down, then you are an illegitimate child.

I beseech you, child, as an elder to a novice, as one who has grown old in my monastic habit, even though I have been useful for nothing, to one who has just been tonsured. May this not be for no reason; no, Lord Jesus Christ; nor let it be in vain! Be vigilant, awaken from the stupor of your heavy sleep, rise up with Peter and the rest of the apostles to cry out to the Savior of all, Christ, with a loud voice: "Master, save us, for we are drowning" (Lk 8.24). And he will surely come to you as well, rebuking the winds and the sea, calming the storm that surrounds your boat, namely the winter of your soul. He will lift you up from the blood-sucking lion, saving your dove from the belly of the beast (cf. Jon 2.2), and your seed from the hail, and your olive tree from the worms, and all your trees from the frost, so that they may give forth fruits in their proper time (cf. Mt 21.41). And the seed of your soil will yield ripe fruit according to the apostolic word: "One hundredfold, and sixty times and thirty times" (Mk 4.8).

Brother, pay attention to why you are enduring this, for God's name. The Apostle has enumerated the reasons: "Who will separate us from the love of Christ? Will hardship, or distress, or persecution, or famine, or nakedness, or peril, or sword?" (Rom 8.35). So can a small illness shake our intellect away from God? Let it not be so! But be strengthened, child, and you will see God's help. For this is but a first temptation, and if you should overcome it with the help of God, then it will no longer dominate you. However, if this overcomes you, it will lead you to a state of enslavement. Therefore, stand strong and endure. For you will certainly see, if you do indeed stand strong, what the Lord's mercy will bring you.

Let your love be reassured that I shall not cease praying to God for you, night and day, in order that he may save you and protect us all from the evil one. And I am striving hard, so that, like the saints, you may as their children inherit "what no eye has seen, nor ear heard, nor the human heart conceived, in regard to what God has prepared for those who love him" (1 Cor 2.9). Pursue these things, and you will be blessed in Christ. Amen.

The power of forgiveness

614. A brother[62] committed a fault, and when the Abbot asked him numerous times merely to say once: "Forgive me!" his heart was hardened and he refused to do so. When the Abbot said a prayer and kneeled three times, he barely convinced him to say: "Forgive me!" So when the brother returned to his own cell, the Abbot said to him: "Brother, when you are alone in your cell, examine your heart, and you will discover whence this hardness came to your heart." When he did this, the brother came and threw himself at the feet of the Abbot, confessing his sin and entreating him to reveal this matter to the Great Old Man Barsanuphius, and to ask him to pray for him.

---

[62]A disobedient brother in the community of Seridos.

The saint addressed the following words in response.

Brother, pay attention to yourself. It was you that asked me to sow seed on your soil; no one obliged you to this. See, then, that you do not allow the devil to sow tares in your harvest, namely the destruction of eternal fire. I am responding to you, since you asked me about your thoughts. The fathers say that, if someone asks about something, then that person should keep those commandments until death; and if any are not kept, then they bring destruction.

You have evil and terrible thoughts lurking in your intellect. Why then do you consider those thoughts as being mortal, which in fact are not? The devil is the one who transforms for you the light into darkness and the darkness into light, as well as the bitter into sweet and the sweet into bitter. So now you see life as death and death as life. For, the enemy wanders about roaring, desiring to swallow you up alive. And yet, you do not understand that, were it not for the hand of God and the prayers of the saints, you would have fallen into the devil's destruction and deceit.

So you reject the divine words spoken by your Abbot, for the benefit and salvation of your soul, so that, as a result, you may never come to the knowledge of truth. You ignore the many labors that he performs for you as if for his own soul, beseeching the saints also to pray for you, so that you may escape from the snares of the devil and of death, and be saved in the nest of the Lord. For, this is how he toils for you.

Should you, then, not keep his words as the apple of your eye (cf. Deut 32.10) and hold him as higher than your own life? Instead, however, you have become vulgar, feeling satiated by his continual presence, something of which you should never have felt satiated but rather prayed to be counted worthy of. Indeed, in order that his continual presence with you may not be to your condemnation, you should have carried out his commands with zeal and great fear and trembling, so that through him you may receive God's blessing and be delivered from the deceit of the enemy.

May the words not be fulfilled in your case: "Jacob ate his fill, and grew fat, and the beloved one kicked" (Deut 32.15). Let not also these words be fulfilled in you: "Woe to you Chorazin! Woe to you Bethsaida! For if the deeds of power done in you had been done in Tyre and Sidon, they would have repented long ago in sackcloth and ashes" (Mt 11.21). And do not be the one to hear: "You hate discipline, and you cast my words behind you" (Ps 49.17).

Why do you put yourself in temptation so often, provoking others with your words and then being unable to bear what they say? Yet your heart is blinded by envy and jealousy, and so you bring turmoil upon yourself. Thus you have often fallen into sin, and smashed your face; and yet your copper forehead is not put to shame and your iron neck is not bent, like brother John told you.

Who has behaved like this and been saved? Cain behaved like this in the beginning, and he received a curse from the Lord's hand (cf. Gen 4). And after him, the giants did too, and they were drowned in the waters of the flood (cf. Gen 6.7). Ham and Esau did too, and were cast out of the holy blessings (cf. Gen 9.27). Pharaoh's heart was hardened, and the water of the Red Sea swallowed him up and drowned him as well as those with him (cf. Ex 14.16–28). Those with Dathan opposed Moses, and the earth swallowed them up, together with their families (cf. Num 16). And if, as the Scripture says, those who oppose the high priest are swallowed up by the earth, then how do you dare to oppose the one who simply tells you to say: "Forgive me!" instead of accepting his decree?

Therefore, you have alienated yourself from God's humility and the fathers' *Discourses*, which say: "In every circumstance, we require humility, being prepared with every deed and with every word to say: 'Forgive me!' "[63] Nevertheless, you heard the Abbot say this so many times, and you did not listen to him. Even when you finally did listen to him, it was not a genuine response, because it was done by necessity and not spoken in repentance and compunction. Until

[63] Abba Isaiah of Scetis, *Ascetic Discourse* 3.

when will you be stiff-necked and uncircumcised in heart (cf. Acts 7.51)? Look, and you will see that no one else is hard. So why do you give the devil a hand and the strength to destroy your soul?

Therefore, be vigilant, my brother, be alert; awaken from the deep sleep and the drunkenness that is without wine, but which possesses you. Where is your humility? Where is your obedience? Where is the cutting off of the will in everything? If you cut off your will in one matter and do not do the same in another, it is clear that even in the one where you did cut it off, there is some other desire that is lurking? For, a submissive person submits in everything; and such a person is carefree about one's salvation, since someone else will give account for him, namely the one to whom one has submitted and to whom one has confided oneself. So, if you want to be saved and to live in heaven and on earth, keep these things and I shall give account for you to God, brother. But if you are neglectful, then you are on your own. Do not cut off your hope; for this is the joy of the devil.

I have persuaded the Abbot to receive you in his embrace, like before. Indeed, he was stunned by your disobedience and inattentiveness; and I have convinced him to accept you, in the fear of God, as a genuine son, not as an illegitimate child (cf. Heb 12.8). You too, however, should entrust yourself to him in everything, according to the fear of God. And the Father and Son and Holy Spirit bear witness to me, that I bear all of your care before God; and he will seek your blood from me, if you do not disobey my words. So make a new beginning from today, assisted by the hand of God. Behold, you are young; guard yourself, and do not give yourself over to foolish talk and useless acquaintances.

May the Lord grant you prudence and strength to hear and practice these things. And if there is anything that you may want to ask me from time to time, I shall not delay in responding with whatever God grants to my mouth, in order to reassure your heart and to tell you whatever is necessary for the salvation of your soul, in Christ Jesus. Amen.

The prayer of the saints

616. The [same] brother[64] was reassured with these words and asked the same great Old Man: Your God-loving mouth told me that a sinner is able to wipe away one's own sins through repentance. What does this mean? Does that person not also require the prayer of the saints? Can that person do this alone? And if such a person does not show sincere repentance, if the saints pray for him, are his sins not wiped away on account of them?

Response by Barsanuphius

If a person does not do whatever one can, and join this effort with the prayer of the saints, then the prayer of the saints is of no benefit to him. If they lead an ascetic life and pray for him, while he leads a life of waste and wantonness, then to what avail is their prayer for him? For, the saying is fulfilled: "When one builds and another tears down, what do they gain but hard work? (Sir 34.28)

Indeed, if it were possible for such a thing to happen, namely for the saints to pray for someone and he would be saved, while the latter was not even a little careful, then nothing would prevent them from doing this for the sins of the whole world. Rather, if a sinner labors even a little, he certainly requires the prayer of the righteous. For, the Apostle says: "The prayer of the righteous is powerful and effective" (Jas 5.16). Therefore, when a saintly and righteous person prays for someone, the sinner should also contribute all that is possible through repentance, again through the prayer of the saints; for, the sinner is entirely incapable of repaying one's debts alone. Moreover, the sinner contributes little, while the prayer of the saints contributes much.

Just like someone who needs to carry ten measures of wheat, but is unable to carry even two, that person will look for another God-fearing person to carry the other nine, in order that he may let him

[64]The same disobedient brother.

carry only the one. In this way, all ten will be preserved; for, he will reach the city without being attacked by thieves on the way. The same may be applied in this case.

Or again, a sinner is like someone who owes one hundred coins, and who is reminded by the lender about the deposit of his debt. And going to another pious person, who is also wealthy, he entreats that person to give as much as possible, according to love. And that loving-kind benefactor sees his affliction and shows compassion, saying: "Brother, whatever I am holding in my hands, I shall give for your sake; however, see that you also give at least ten coins from your own pocket; for, I have ninety coins, and I will give them to you in order to relieve you of your debt." So it is up to the debtor to strive to give a little in order to be freed from much. For, if that compassionate benefactor sees that the debtor has not brought forward the ten coins, then he hesitates to give the ninety, knowing that the original lender will not wipe away the debt unless he receives the hundred coins that are owed.

On almsgiving and perfection

617. A Christ-loving person[65] asked the Other Old Man, John: I beseech you, father, clarify this for me, so that I may depart joyfully. Since my thought is telling me to offer some alms from my possessions, what is it beneficial for me to do? Should I give things away gradually, or should I give them away once for all?

Response by John

Brother, even if I am not capable of responding to you as I should, yet you have the counsel of Scripture: "Do not say: 'Go, and come again tomorrow, I will give it,' when you have it with you now. For

---

[65]A devout layman. *Letters* 617–773 are addressed to various laypersons in the surrounding region. Most of the responses are by Abba John.

you do not know what the morrow will bring" (Prov 3.28). More-over, there are particular measures, and each person acts according to their own measure. For one person is able to give away only some of his income, while another person will tithe his fruits, or else gives away one-quarter, or a third, or even half; each one gives according to their own measure.

If anyone wants to come to the measure of perfection, that person should not ask me, the least of all, but rather the teacher and healer of souls, Jesus the Lord, who said to that rich man: "If you wish to be perfect, go sell your possessions, and give the money to the poor, and you will have treasure in heaven; then come, follow me" (Mt 19.21).

The presence of death also strengthens your thought; for it is concealed from all people. Therefore, let us strive to do what is good before we are seized before the hour of death—for we do not know on what day we shall be called—lest we be found to be unprepared and be shut out with the five foolish bridesmaids, who did not take flasks with their lamps (cf. Mt 25.1–13). Let us do our best according to our weakness, and the Master of all is good; he shall allow us to enter with the wise bridesmaids into his wedding-chamber and into the ineffable joy that is with Christ. Amen.

Almsgiving and monasticism

618. A brother asked the same Old Man whether he should receive money from others in order to give to the poor; for some people are requesting this.

Response by John

Since we are on the subject of almsgiving, not everyone can bear the application of this virtue, but only those who have reached silence and are mourning for their own sins. For there are some who commit themselves to such a service, and God knows what to do with them in this regard. However, those who mourn[66] are not pre-occupied with almsgiving. For how is it possible, when they have renounced their own possessions, for them to manage the posses-sions of others?

This is what St Hilarion did. When someone entreated him to accept a large amount of money and to distribute this to the poor, he said to that person: "You should be distributing your own money; for you are the one traveling from city to city, and you are familiar with the towns. Whereas I, who have left behind my own property, cannot possibly accept to distribute the property of another. Indeed, this can give rise to an excuse for vainglory or avarice."

Almsgiving and society

619. *Question.* If the one who is proposing this insists, saying: "If you do not accept the money and distribute it to the poor, then I will not offer it," should I allow the poor to suffer hunger?

Response.[67]

As I told your love, there are some that have committed themselves to this service of almsgiving. However, if you want to mourn for your sins, do not pay any attention to this matter, even if you see someone dying before your very cell. Do not take part in the distri-bution of another's possessions and be distracted from your mourn-ing. Nevertheless, the owner of the property should distribute the goods himself, if he cannot find someone else to perform this serv-ice, so that in this way the work is not hindered.

---

[66]That is, the monastics.
[67]By Abba John.

Almsgiving and poverty

620. A Christ-loving layperson asked the same Old Man: If someone is asked to give alms but has nothing to give, is that person obliged to borrow in order to give?

Response by John

If someone is asked to give something that one does not have, then there is no need to borrow in order to give. For even the Apostle Peter was asked to give alms and responded: "I have no silver or gold" (Acts 3.6); and he did not borrow any money in order to give. Indeed, even if one only has the bare necessities, then again there is no need to spend it all, so that one may not miss it later and be afflicted by its absence.

And if the person from whom alms are demanded says: "Forgive me; for I have nothing to give you," then this is not a lie. Indeed, someone who has nothing beyond what is needed does not have anything to give to another person. He should simply say to the person who is asking: "Forgive me, but I only have what I need myself." Remember the five bridesmaids who asked of the others to give them oil for their lamps; the latter replied: "There will not be enough for us and for you" (Mt 25.9). And the Apostle Paul writes in his letter to the Corinthians: "May your abundance be for their need" (2 Cor 8.14), as well as: "I do not mean that there should be relief for others and pressure on you" (2 Cor 8.13).

Almsgiving with discernment

621. *Question* from the same person to the same Old Man: Father, tell me what you meant when you said: "If someone only has the bare necessities, then there is no need to spend it all in order not to be afflicted." How is it possible for someone to be afflicted when one does something voluntarily?

Response by John

One should do everything with discernment. To know one's limits is discernment as well as security of thought, in order not to be troubled later. Doing anything beyond one's measure, whether this be almsgiving or anything else, is lack of discernment. For this later brings one to turmoil, despondency, and murmuring. So, it is a good thing, indeed a very good thing, to give like the widow to anyone who asks; there is nothing wrong with this. But as for a person giving more than one can possibly bear, even God only asks only for what one can give.

Levels of almsgiving

622. *Question.* So are you saying that someone who is wealthy and has more than the bare necessities does not require this discernment? For, that person too acts according to his ability.

Response by John

No, such a person, too, requires discernment, in order not to be found to act beyond the ability of his thought and then regret what he has done. This is why Paul also said: "Do not give out of sorrow or necessity; for God loves a joyful giver" (2 Cor 9.7). However, the perfect measures are for the perfect, and the lesser measures are for the lesser. The perfect person bears even poverty with courage, scorning wealth and bearing everything calmly, according to the Apostle: "I can do all things through him who strengthens me" (Phil 4.13), and: "For me, the world has been crucified" (Gal 6.14), and so on.

Learning to give alms

623. *Question.* What should someone do to become accustomed to giving alms, if from the beginning one does not enjoy giving at all?

Response by John

That person should remind oneself how God will reward those who give, and begin with small things, always advising oneself that one who gives little will receive little; one who gives much will also receive much, according to the words: "The one who sows sparingly will also reap sparingly; and the one who sows bountifully will also reap bountifully" (2 Cor 9.6). And, from the little, the thought is gradually moved to desire the bountiful, and therefore always progresses toward perfection. Such a person can reach perfect measures, in order to render oneself naked of all earthly things and become one in spirit with the heavenly things.

Almsgiving and economy

625. *Question.* If there happen to be two poor persons, and I do not have enough money for both, which of the two should I prefer?

Response by John

You should prefer the weaker one.

Almsgiving and stinginess

626. *Question.* If I would like to give alms, but my thought has doubts about giving, what should I do?

Response by John

Examine yourself, and if you find that you are doing this out of stinginess, then give something even beyond what you should have given, for example an additional small amount, and you will receive God's mercy.

Almsgiving and salvation

627. *Question.* Abba sir, clarify this for me as well. How is it possible for someone who has nothing to give to become a partaker of the blessing expressed by the Savior to those on his right: "Come, you that are blessed by my Father, inherit the kingdom prepared for you from the foundation of the world; for I was hungry and you gave me to eat" (Mt 25.34–35), and so forth?

Response by John

Brother, is it possible that the Apostles, who did not have any possessions, are not partakers of this blessing? For, there are various ranks of people, and God has spoken to each person according to his own rank. He demonstrated through the Beatitudes how those who are saved are distinguished into various ranks. So from material examples, one may grasp the spiritual meanings.

Suppose, for example, that one person has fresh vegetables and sells some of them, in order to purchase a small coin of gold. Someone else, who owns other goods, will sell those in order to purchase the same gold coin. The same occurs with the various professions; one person is a carpenter and earns a small amount of gold each day, while another is a constructor and earns a similar amount each day. Someone else has a different profession and again earns the same salary each day. Therefore, the various professions are different, and the results of each also differ; but the cost and salary are the same.

Now let us apply this in order to understand what occurs in the case of the soul. It is to those who have money and who give to the poor without vainglory that these words are addressed: "Come, you that are blessed by my Father, inherit the kingdom prepared for you from the foundation of the world; for I was hungry, and you gave me to eat" (Mt 25.34–35), and so on. Nevertheless, pay attention to the rest of the Beatitudes, and you will discover a great difference in the ways that they are proposed; for one speaks of the salvation of the soul, and another of the heavenly kingdom. Therefore, he said: "Blessed are the poor in spirit; for theirs is the kingdom of heaven" (Mt 5.3). And again: "Blessed are those who are persecuted for righteousness' sake; for theirs is the kingdom of heaven" (Mt 5.10). The other Beatitudes too are different to these, but do not differ greatly in regard to the reward, which is the kingdom of heaven.

So, if you have nothing in order to give alms, then become poor in spirit, in order that you may inherit, with the saints, the kingdom of heaven. Mourn over your sins in this world, in order that you may be comforted with those whose names are written in the Gospel. Acquire meekness, in order that you may inherit the earth. Hunger and thirst after righteousness, in order that you may be filled with the same. Be pure in heart, in order that you may see God in his glory. Become a peacemaker in your heart, in order that you may be called a child of God. Be prepared through your good deeds to be persecuted for the sake of righteousness, from city to city, namely from the evil thought of the devil to the good thought of God, in order that you may rejoice in the inheritance of the kingdom of heaven. Endure reproach and persecution and false witness for the sake of the Lord, in order that you may be gladdened; for you will discover that great is the reward in heaven.

Beatitudes and virtues

628. *Question* from the same person to the same Old Man: since each of the Beatitudes contains one virtue, is this one virtue sufficient, father, for salvation, should a person acquire it?

Response by John

Just as the body is one but has many members, and if one member is missing, then the body is not complete, you should understand the inner person in the same way too. For, the inner person has many members, namely many virtues, and if one of these is missing, then one cannot be perfected. It is like a craftsman, who knows his profession well, may also be able to handle other crafts too on account of his skills, yet he is not called a craftsman except of his own profession. The same applies to every person in the spiritual life. For, one needs to have all the virtues, but will be recognized by and reputed for one particular virtue, through which the grace of the Spirit especially shines.

On buying and selling

648. *Question.* There is a garden at some distance from where I live that belongs to my nephews, and some people have decided to purchase it in order to build a place of prayer. My nephews charged me to deal with them in regard to the price of the garden. However, I am seized by two thoughts: one tells me that I should give it to them at no cost, since it will be used as a sacred place; another tells me to keep the charge entrusted to me by those who asked me to settle a price. And I do not know on which side to lean. For I fear God; but I also think I should not harm my nephews. What, then, should I do, father?

Response by Barsanuphius

Declare to them the fair price of the garden, entreating them and saying: "You know that we are all indebted to our masters, the saints. So whatever the Lord inspires you to contribute, perhaps lowering the price a little, it is up to you." Put this in writing. It is then up to them to do so or not, and you cannot be blamed about the matter. For it is not an onerous sin to demand a fair price, even if it happens to be for a house of the Lord. However, it is beneficial also for the one who owns and controls the garden, if that person is not poor, to lower the price as much possible, since it is for a house of God; for that person will receive abundance in fruits as a result of this. However, if the owner is unable to lower the price, God will not demand anything more than a good intention.

When he heard these things, he left rejoicing and glorifying God.

On hiring and firing

653. Another Christ-loving layperson had a servant who was not useful, who left at one point and then returned again after a while. He asked the Old Man, John, whether he should keep this servant. However, after the Old Man had declared to him that he should be released, the servant began to show good conduct and so that person was grieved about releasing him. So he sent off again asking about this matter, namely whether he should release him.

Response by John

Keep your servant for the time being, testing both him as well as yourself through him. And if he should be corrected, then it is all well and good. However, if he persists in the same conduct, and you keep him for the sake of God, this too is fine; for you will receive the reward of patience. However, if you see that you cannot tolerate him, but instead you are coming to be harmed on account of him, then release him so that he may leave. Remember one of the saints, who said: "If you see someone drowning in the river, do not reach out your hand to him, in case he drags you, too, into the water; but stretch out your staff to him. If you are able to save him by using your staff, then well and good. But if you cannot save him, then let go of your staff, so that you also are not drowned with him."[68]

Problems in employment

654. Some days later, the servant tried to tempt his master by stealing something, but the Lord protected the master and the servant ended up leaving. So his master came to thank the Other Old Man for this protection, blaming himself that, after the first response, he nevertheless still delayed in releasing the servant.

The Old Man declared the following to him.

It was not with the purpose of expelling him that I told you to release the servant, but on account of the weakness of your thought. For, you could not endure being tempted by him. After all, we are sinners, and it is not up to us to expel anyone. Had you been able to keep him in spite of his laziness, you would have received your reward on his account.

For, indeed, some of the fathers used to say about Abba Poemen, that he kept his disciple in spite of his laziness. And Abba Poemen said: "If I could, I would place a pillow under his head." And they said: "Then, what would you say to God?" And he replied: "I would say to God: 'You are the one who said, Hypocrite, first remove the log from your own eye, and then you will see clearly to take out the speck from your neighbor's eye' " (Mt 7.5).[69]

[68] *Sayings*, Poemen 92.
[69] *Sayings*, Poemen 117.

On judgment, counsel and humility

655. *Question.* So did that Abba do the right thing in not correcting his brother?

Response by John

Brother, it is not by chance that the Abba stopped counseling him; instead, he advised him on many occasions, but the latter did not accept the advice. Therefore, seeing that the brother was not taking to correction, he left the matter to the judgment of God, saying: "God knows what is beneficial; for my brother is much better than I." This is what the perfect used to do; for they did not dare to judge anyone, putting to shame those who are nothing and yet still judge everyone.

Discipline with compassion

656. *Question.* When my servant makes a mistake and I want to discipline him, with what purpose should I do this?

Response by John

With the purpose of love, that is according to God, so that by being corrected through your discipline, he may cease to sin and so that this may occur for the salvation of his soul. Yet, you should not do this with anger; for, nothing good comes out of evil. Therefore, if your thought is troubled, wait until it calms down. And, in this way, you will discipline him with compassion in godly fear.

Discipline with humility

657. *Question.* But when I want to discipline him, my thought tells me: "You do worse things than he; why do you discipline him when you do not correct yourself?"

Response by John

This thought comes from the devil, in order that the brother may remain uncorrected and you may give account for him. Say to your thought: "It is true that I commit greater sins—that is evident, and I recognize it—but I am unable to give account both for me and for him; for God will demand of me his correction." And, after you have disciplined him carefully and with fear of God, repeat to yourself the words of the Apostle: "You that teach others, do you not teach yourself?" (Rom 2.21). In this way, you will be found to discipline him with humility.

Responding to those who insult religion

658. *Question.* When I see someone insulting religion and blaspheming the holy faith, I am troubled against this person, supposedly out of zeal. What does this mean?

Response by John

You have certainly heard that no one can come to correction through evil, but rather only through good. Therefore, speak to this person with meekness and long-suffering, advising him in godly fear. And if you see that you are troubled, it is not necessary to say anything to him.

On promotions

664. Another Christ-loving layperson, who was a professor of secular wisdom, asked the Great Old Man, whether he would do well in accepting a promotion.

He responded the following.

Do not feel arrogant, and you shall find grace from God and among people, as well as enjoy great success wherever you happen to be.

Again on promotions

665. The same person asked the Other Old Man about this.

Response by John

God has always chosen the humble. Have humility, and God will assist you quickly.

On resorting to the law

669. *Question.* Father, what happens if someone comes to take my cloak? Should I give it to him at once? For how many such evil and wicked people exist, who would gladly do this, to the point of even leaving someone naked, if they could?

Response by Barsanuphius

This is not said in order that whoever simply wants to take something from you may receive it from you. Rather, it is said for the one who wants to sue you, which signifies inhumanness, as well as for the courts which bring harm to the soul. Therefore, in that case, one should scorn fleshly things in light of the salvation of the soul. For it is said: "What will it profit them, if they gain the whole world but forfeit their life?" (Mt 16.26).

On consulting lawyers

670. *Question.* Since there are some who are familiar with the court system, and they are not harmed as much as those who are unfamiliar, is it good to handle such legal matters through them?

Response by Barsanuphius

Even if they are familiar with the courts, yet it is we who would be responsible for adding such harm to them. Nevertheless, in comparing the two evils, the latter is no less harmful; for when we instigate this procedure, we are brought to the destruction of our soul. However, if they too are being harmed like we, then we are responsible for their harm; that sin will weigh down on us, and we shall bear the harm. For it is written: "The evil is bound to come, but woe to anyone by whom it comes" (Lk 17.1).

Now, if someone is not satisfied with the conclusions of the court, but strives to make his accused suffer greater evils, then this is the worst of all, and it angers God still more. For he said: "Do not repay evil for evil" (1 Pet 3.9), and: "Forgive, that you may be forgiven" (Mt 6.14).

On testifying in court

671. *Question.* If it is necessary to bear witness about a murder that really happened, should one lie in order that the murderer may escape death?

Response by Barsanuphius

If you never lie, then you should not lie in this either. For it is written: "Do not be compassionate to a poor person who is being judged" (Ex 23.3). If it is not the will of God, then that person will not die. However, if you lie in other circumstances and you will want to lie in this case as well, then do as you usually do. For it is written: "Anyone who commits sin is also guilty of lawlessness" (1 Jn 3.4). As for me, I have nothing to say on this. However, if it is not necessary for you to bear witness, then you need not say anything at all. For there is a useful proverb here: "Saying: 'I do not know' places no one in prison."

On lending money

672. *Question.* If one has debtors who are wealthy, should one demand interest from these people? And if they are poor, should one even take back the capital?

Response by John

It is written of the righteous: "They do not lend their money with interest" (Ps 15.5). This means that we may receive the capital. Now, if some of them are unable to pay it back, it has also been written about them: "When your friends are in poverty, do not distress them by making demands of them" (Sir 31.31).

On repaying loans

673. *Question.* What happens if both he and I are poor? Am I committing sin by demanding what I need?

Response by Barsanuphius

No, you are not committing sin. However, it is good not to distress one's brother, as much as this is possible, if he is too poor to repay us.

On being mistreated

679. Another Christ-loving layperson was greatly mistreated by someone, and told the Great Old Man about this.

And the Old Man said the following.

Do good to him.

Again on being mistreated

680. After doing this, he was still greatly mistreated by him, and once again declared this to the Great Old Man, saying: Behold, I am doing good to him, but he does not stop doing evil to me.

And the Old Man said the following.

You are not actually doing anything good to him, but only to yourself; for, the Lord said: "Do good to your enemies, and pray for those who mistreat you" (Lk 6.27–28). So each person will receive according to his own work.

On relations with non-Christians

686. Another Christ-loving layperson asked the same Old Man: I want to press some Jewish wine in my presser. Is this a sin?

Response by John

If, when God rains, it rains in your field but not in that of the Jew, then do not press his wine. If he is loving-kind to all and rains upon the just and the unjust (cf. Mt 5.45), then why do you want to be inhumane and not compassionate, rather, as he says: "Be merciful, even as your Father in heaven is merciful" (Lk 6.36).

On discussing doctrine

694. *Question.* If I am sitting among certain fathers and have doubts about the faith of one of them, that he is not thinking correctly, should I participate in the conversation as well or not? For my thought tells me that if I am silent, I am betraying the faith. And if they are having a simple conversation about doctrinal matters, should I say what I know, or keep silent? And if I am asked, then what should I do?

Response by John

Never take part in conversations about the faith; for God will not demand this of you. God will only ask whether you believe correctly what you have received from the holy Church at the time of your baptism and whether you keep his commandments. Therefore, maintain these things, and you shall be saved.

Furthermore, it is not necessary to talk about doctrines; for this is beyond you. Rather, pray to God for all your sins, and let your intellect spend time on related matters. See, however, that you do not condemn within your heart those who do talk about doctrines; for you do not know whether they are speaking correctly or not; nor do you know how God will judge the matter. So, if you are asked, simply say: "These things are beyond me; forgive me, holy fathers."

Authority to teach

695. *Question.* If the heretic is arguing better than the Orthodox brother during this discussion, is it then good perhaps for me to support the latter as much as I can, lest he be harmed in the Orthodox faith by losing the debate?

Response by John

If you enter into the conversation, and speak before God and people, then you are seen to be as one who is teaching. And, if one teaches without having the authority to do so, then one's words are not inspired by God but remain fruitless. So, if there is no benefit in your speaking, why is it necessary to speak at all?

However, if you truly want to help, speak within your heart to the God who knows our secrets, and who is able to achieve more than we could ask for. And he will deal with those who are debating, in accordance with his will, while you will find humility through this.

It is like someone who imprisons another person by force and without just reason. When a third person sees what has happened, although he cannot do or say anything in opposition, yet he may go secretly to a more powerful person, who will send for the first person's release by his own authority. Meanwhile, the one who imprisoned that man is troubled, because he does not know who reported it. The same also applies here.

Let us approach God with prayer of heart for our faith and for our brothers, and he who swore unto himself: "that he desires all people to be saved and to come to the knowledge of truth" (1 Tim 2.4) and life will do with them likewise, according to his will.

Do not meddle

696. *Question.* Should I ask to learn what they are discussing in order to be sure?

Response by John

Ask about nothing that God will not demand from you. Nor contribute any dangerous words. But be satisfied, as I have already told you, with the confession of the correct faith, and do not meddle in anything else beyond this.

Silence is always better

697. *Question.* If, however, the discussion is about the Scriptures, should I keep silent or may I speak? And if they happen to be unsure about something, about which I do know, is it perhaps good for me to speak then or not?

Response by John

Silence is the better. However, if they are unsure about something, and you know about this, then in order to solve their doubt, speak what you know with humility. But if you do not know, then do not say anything from your own thought; for, this is foolishness.

Speak when spoken to

698. *Question.* If the conversation is about various matters, which are not harmful to the soul, should I keep silent or speak?

Response by John

It is not good to speak before being asked. If you are asked to say something, say what you know in humility and fear of God. Neither feel arrogant if your words are accepted, not feel grieved if your words are not accepted. For, this is the way of God. And, in order that you are not considered as having the gift of silence, say something of your own in knowledge, but be brief and avoid too many words and inopportune glory.

Do not hurry to condemn heretics

699. *Question.* If someone asks me to anathematize Nestorius and the heretics with him, should I do this or not?

Response by John

That Nestorius and those heretics who follow him are under anathema, this is clear. But you should not hurry to anathematize anyone at all. For one who regards himself as sinful should mourn over one's sins, and do nothing else. Neither, however, should you judge those who anathematize someone; for each person tests oneself.

Heresy and self-awareness

700. *Question.* But if one thinks, as a result of this, that I believe the same as Nestorius, what should I tell him?

Response by John

Tell him: "Although it is clear that those people were worthy of their anathema, nevertheless I am more sinful than every other person, and fear that, in judging another, I may condemn myself. Indeed, even if I anathematize Satan himself, if I am doing his works, then I am anathematizing myself.

"For, the Lord said: 'If you love me, you will keep my commandments' (Jn 14.15). And the Apostle says: 'Whosoever does not love the Lord, let that person be under anathema' (1 Cor 16.22). Therefore, one who does not keep his commandments does not love him; and one who does not love him, is under anathema. So, then, how can such a person anathematize others?" Say these things to him; and if he persists in this, then for the sake of his conscience, just anathematize the heretic!

Conversation and prayer

707. *Question.* If I am sitting with some secular people and they begin idle talk, should I stay or depart? And if it is necessary for me to stay, then what should I do?

Response by John

If it is not necessary for you to stay, then depart; if it is indeed necessary for you to stay, then transfer your intellect to prayer, without condemning the others, but realizing your own weakness.

Topics of conversation

708. *Question.* And if they happen to be my beloved ones, do you decree that I transfer this conversation to another topic that is more useful?

Response by John

If you know that they would gladly receive the word of God, then speak from the *Lives of the Fathers*, and transfer the topic of conversation to the salvation of the soul.

Conversation and temptation

709. *Question.* So is it good to invoke the name of God when in conversation with someone?

Response by John

It is necessary to invoke the name of God both during conversation with someone and before such conversation, as well as after the conversation, and indeed at every time and in every place. For, it is written: "Pray unceasingly" (1 Thess 5.17). This is how every temptation is abolished.

On praying without ceasing

710. *Question.* And how is it possible for someone to pray unceasingly?

Response by John

When one is alone, one should recite the Psalms and pray with one's mouth and one's heart. However, when one is in the marketplace, or with other people, it is not necessary to recite the Psalms with one's mouth, but only with one's mind. It is also necessary to guard one's eyes and to lower them, on account of the distraction and snares of the enemies.

The power of prayer

711. *Question.* When I pray or recite the Psalms, I do not understand the meaning of the words on account of the hardness of my heart. Of what benefit are they to me?

Response by John

Even if you do not understand the meaning of the words, yet the demons understand it and hear it and tremble at it. Therefore, do not cease reciting the Psalms and praying; and gradually, God will soften the hardness.

On praying at meal-times

715. *Question.* If I am sharing a meal with some of the fathers, and one of them has already blessed the food at the table, should I first say: "Bless me!" before eating, and wait for him to bless me again, or should I be satisfied with the first blessing? Because, sometimes his mind happens to be elsewhere and he delays in responding, and I am always grieved. Or is it perhaps good enough for me to make the sign of the Cross over the food that I am about to eat?

Response by John

He has blessed the food once, and this is more than enough. As far as making the sign of the Cross, this too is not necessary. For the blessing is a seal in itself. In fact, you would be giving occasion for the one who blessed the food or, indeed, for any other person present, to think that you do not trust his blessing; and this will cause a scandal.

On blessing the meal

717. *Question.* If all of us around the table are laypersons, what should we do when we do not have anyone to bless the food?

Response by John

It is a good thing for laypersons to bless God when they are about to eat. For the food is blessed through the remembrance of God. However, this blessing is unlike that of the clergy; it is merely a doxology and remembrance of God. Yet, it is fitting that everyone remembers God and glorifies him. Therefore, it is good for laypersons to do this as well, when they have no one else to bless the food.

On who should bless the food

718. *Question.* If, nevertheless, they hesitate as to who should bless the food first, since each of them gives priority to the other, what should be done?

Response by John

The one who invited them should also invite whomever he wants to bless the table, and that person should bless. If no one accepts, in order to avoid any argument, then the host should accept himself, and say: "Through the prayers of the holy fathers, may God be with us. Amen."

On settling legal disputes

725. Another Christ-loving layperson asked the same Old Man, saying: I have a legal matter with someone. What do you order me

to do? Should I claim strict justice with him or should I ignore strict justice for the sake of finishing sooner?

Response by John

Strive, to the best of your ability, to be reconciled quickly; for it is a sign of the perfect not to be troubled by the temptations that come upon them. However, the weak person, who is unable to resist the temptation, later happens to regret the matter; then, instead of coming to himself, he turns to blaspheme against God and loses his soul. Thus, the following words are fulfilled in him: "For what does it profit a person to gain the whole world and forfeit his life?" (Mk 8.36).

Mercy and justice

726. *Question.* Someone owes me money, and unless I ignore this a little, we shall never come to have peace. What do you order me to do?

Response by John

Whoever seeks peace is not deprived of God's peace. "Whoever is faithful in very little is faithful also in much" (Lk 16.10); and: "Mercy triumphs over judgment" (Jas 2.13). Therefore, unless a person despises the needs of the world, that person does not attain to the peace of Christ. "The one who began a good work among you will bring it to completion by the day of Jesus Christ" (Phil 1.6). For this is our prayer: that God may grant us peace, so that we may complete the work of God, as the most holy Guest-Master of the entire Church bore witness.

On leaving church early

736. *Question.* If one enters the church during the time of liturgy and leaves before the end, is this a sin?

Response by John

What is perfect and pleasing to God is for the person entering the church to hear the Scriptures and remain in the liturgy until the very end. For unless there is good reason, one should not leave before the end; for this is scornful. If some need presents itself, then that person has permission to leave early. However, even then, such a person should not justify oneself, but ask forgiveness from God, saying: "Master, forgive me; for, I was not able to stay."

On silence in church

737. *Question.* Should one speak in church or not?

Response by John

One should not speak at all in the house of God during the divine liturgy, but rather spend time in prayer and listening attentively to the sacred Scriptures; for, they speak of things necessary for the salvation of our souls. Nevertheless, if it is necessary to speak, one should be brief out of respect and fear for the hour at hand, also regarding the matter as being to our condemnation.

On speaking in church

738. *Question.* If I do not want to speak but some of the fathers, who are present, begin speaking to me, what should I do in order

that they may not be scandalized by my silence, thinking that it is a matter of scorn?

Response by John

If they begin speaking to you, then respond briefly, regarding this matter too as being to your condemnation.

When financial resources are tight

744. *Question.* My thought suggests to me that my material resources are tight and that I cannot feed myself or my household, and this causes me sorrow. What does this mean?

Response by John

This sorrow is human; for, if we had hope in God, he would provide for us as he wants. "Therefore, cast your concern upon the Lord" (1 Pet 5.7), and he is able to take care of you and your own without sorrow and affliction. Say to him: "Your will be done" (Mt 6.10 and 26.42), and he will not allow you to grieve or be afflicted. May the Lord have mercy upon you and protect you with his right hand. Amen.

On settling financial accounts

750. *Question.* If I settle an account and afterward discover that I tricked my brother without wanting to, what should I do?

Response by John

If the amount is large, then return it to him. If it is small, then examine your thought carefully, asking—from the contrary perspective—

what you would do if you were tricked by him and were about to receive that amount; if you find that you would indeed want to receive it, then you too should return it. If you would not receive it, then neither should you give it, unless the person was extremely poor; for in this case, a small amount would make a difference. In that case, you should give him what is fair.

Working on a Sunday

751. *Question.* Is it really a sin to work on a Sunday?

Response by John

For those who work according to God, it is not a sin; indeed, the Apostle said: "I worked night and day, so that I might not burden any of you" (1 Thess 2.9). For those who work in scorn, greed, and shameful gain, it is a sin. Nevertheless, it is a good thing to stop all work and to attend church on the Resurrection day, on the major feasts of the Lord and the memorial days of the Apostles. For, this is a tradition from the holy Apostles.

On settling on a price

756. *Question.* If one is buying or selling something, is it a sin to agree on a price, which is higher or lower?

Response by John

If there is no constraint but the matter is handled in freedom, then it is not a sin to give and take according to the agreed price. However, if one knows that one has gained more, then one should return the amount of one's own accord; for, one will be doing something good and will also be pleasing the other person.

When one agrees on a price with someone that is under one's authority, then one should also examine whether the agreement was made by force; for this is a sin. Rather, one should reassure the other person, by saying: "Brother, I shall not grieve if you do not do as I say; nor shall I offer you more. Therefore, do as you please and as you want."

On concealing the truth partially

758. *Question.* If I do something against my brother and he grieves upon hearing about it, is it perhaps a good thing to hide the truth from him in order to stop the grief? Or is it better to admit my fault and ask for forgiveness?

Response by John

If he has clearly learned about it, and you know that the matter will be examined and revealed, then tell him the truth and ask for his forgiveness. For lying will only further provoke him. However, if he has not learned about it and will not examine the matter, then it is not improper to keep silent and not give occasion to grief.

For when the Prophet Samuel was sent to anoint David as king, he was also going to offer sacrifice to God. Yet, because he was afraid lest Saul learn about this, God said to him: "Take a heifer with you; and if the king asks you: 'Why did you come here?' tell him: 'I have come to sacrifice to the Lord' " (1 Sam 16.2). In this way, by concealing one thing, which brought the wrath of the king, he only revealed the other.

You too, then, should be silent about that which causes grief, and the problem will pass.

On always assuming responsibility

759. *Question.* If it is clear that I did not hurt a person, but instead was hurt by that person, how am I supposed to blame myself? What happens, for example, if I am traveling somewhere and come across someone along the way, whom I do not know at all and who beats me without reason, without me saying anything to him? How can I blame myself in this case?

Response by John

You can say: "It is my fault for coming this way; had I not come this way, I would not have met this man and would not have been beaten by him." Do you see, now, that you can ascribe the fault to yourself?

On always blaming oneself

760. *Question.* If I neither see the sin as being apparent nor is it clear to me immediately how I should blame myself, what should I do?

Response by John

Well, then, say: "It is clear that I am at fault; however, the sin is now concealed from me." That is how you can blame yourself.

On free will

763. A Christ-loving layperson asked the same Old Man: "God created the human person free, but he also says: 'Without me, you are not able to do anything' (Jn 15.5). How, then, is this freedom reconciled with not being able to do anything without God?"

Response by John

God created the human person free in order that we may be able to incline toward good; yet, even while inclining out of freedom, we are incapable of accomplishing this without the assistance of God. For it is written: "It depends not on human will or exertion, but on God who shows mercy" (Rom 9.16).

Therefore, if we incline the heart toward good and invoke God to our assistance, God will pay attention to our good intention and bestow strength upon our work. In this way, both are developed, namely human freedom and God's power. For this is how good comes about, but it is accomplished through his saints. Thus, God is glorified in all and again glorifies them.

On responsibility for others

765. *Question.* I have a servant who is wounded with leprosy. Should I keep him or not?

Response by John

It is not necessary for you to keep him in your house; for not everyone will bear to live with him. If they could bear this, that would be a pious thing to do. Yet, you should not afflict others on his account. Instead, send him to a hospice for poor lepers, and provide for his meals and as many garments as he requires, as well as his bed, so that he is in no way burdened.

On enjoying foods

773. *Question.* Since every food contains a natural sweetness, is this spiritually harmful to the person who eats of it?

Response by John

God our Master created this sweetness in each food, and there is no harm in eating of this with thanksgiving. However, one should always guard against attachment; for this is what is harmful to the soul.

Qualities of a bishop

789. A certain assistant bishop asked the same Old Man whether he should leave his episcopal duties and withdraw to a monastery.

Response by John

I cannot advise you to abandon the one who entrusted you with the care of the holy Churches of God, but only to pay attention to your soul according to the fear of God. Do not accept gifts from anyone; do not waver in your judgment; do not be ashamed in the presence of any ruler in order to find the guilty innocent and condemn the innocent. Keep avarice far from you; for it is the root of all evils. Indeed, this is said to be—and is—a second kind of idolatry. Do not be arrogant, so that you may learn from the Apostle, who says: "Do not be haughty, but associate with the lowly" (Rom 12.16). Do not try to please people; after all, you know what happens to those who do this. They are estranged from the service of Christ; for the Apostle says: "If I were still pleasing people, I would not be a servant of Christ" (Gal 1.10).

Submit to the Lord, who says: "Learn from me; for, I am gentle and humble in heart, and you will find rest for your souls" (Mt 11.29). Quench your anger; for this leads to one's fall. Do everything according to God, and you shall find assistance in him. Always fear death; for we shall surely all die. "Remember the hour of your departure, and you will not sin unto God" (Sir 7.36). And if you arrive at the point of silence, then you shall find rest with grace wherever you may happen to withdraw.

On whom to ordain

805. The same person[70] asked the Other Old Man: Father, whom should I ordain to the priesthood, and what sort of life should they lead?

Response by John

You should ordain people who are worthy of God and good in character, in order that these might minister at the sacred altars of God; they should especially be recommended by many other people, according to the Scripture (1 Tim 3.7).

It is such people that you should strive to ordain, admonishing them upon ordination that God will demand the judgment of the Church from them, should they depart from it. In so doing, you are also showing God your intention and desire to ordain good people for the Churches of God.

Advice for ordination

806. *Question.* If certain holy fathers recommend someone for ordination, should I not be satisfied with their testimony, or should I still demand the approval of the many?

Response by John

You should be satisfied with the testimony of the fathers; for they are speaking in accordance with the will of God and that is how God

[70]A newly-ordained bishop. *Letters* 805 to 844 are addressed to bishops.

desires his ministers. Now, if after receiving such a testimony, you
notice that your thought is troubled, then this tare is sown by the
devil.

Counsel for ordinands

807. *Question.* What happens, then, if, after the testimony of the
fathers, the candidate resigns from receiving ordination or leaves
upon his ordination?

Response [by John]

If the candidate resigns from ordination, then he must be forced to
ordination. If, after being forced, he still leaves, then this does not
constitute cause for blaming those who gave their testimony about
him; it is, however, cause for blaming the candidate for abandoning
the will of God. For, he is obliged to test and labor in the matter.

Then, if he should see that he is incapable, he should again ask
the saints about this, after being salted by the grace of God, and he
should do whatever they tell him. After all, many of the saints
resigned from candidacy to ordination but were obliged by God to
accept. Even Moses said: "Send someone else" (Ex 4.13); and Jere-
miah said: "Truly, I do not know how to speak, for, I am only a boy"
(Jer 1.6).

Other fathers, too, fled from ordination. Yet, once forcefully
seized and ordained, they bore their ministry for the name of God.
However, one who is obliged to come to ordination and then resigns,
is avoiding obedience; and the Scripture says: "Obedience is better
than sacrifice" (1 Sam 15.22).

Now, if someone is considering others, who lead a life of solitude
and meet no person at all, one should not think about ordination for
these people, obliging them to come into the midst of society. However, if there is someone who does meet with other people and will

not reject an invitation to visit towns and cities, whenever there is such a need, if this person is also recommended as being good and skillful, then it is precisely such persons whom the bishops should seize for ordination. For, these are able to benefit not only their own souls but also the souls of others.

This is why the Apostle ordered Titus: "Appoint presbyters in every city" (Titus 1.5), namely to appoint those who were worthy of such a task, such as Titus was. St Gregory, too, and others like him, were ordained by force. Indeed, if we should examine, we shall also discover many other servants of God, even in our own times, who did the same. Nevertheless, although they were greatly afflicted, they endured the labor, fearing that they might reject the will of God.

If someone resigns from his candidacy to ordination without any consideration, then that person needs to pray that his resignation does not afflict his own soul. For it sometimes happens that, for the sake of some pretense to rights, Satan will trip up a person. May the Lord abolish Satan far from our souls and from all those who fear him. Amen.

On keeping church accounts

828. *Question.* Is it a good thing to keep the accounts of a church?

Response by Barsanuphius

If you keep the accounts of the church, you are actually keeping the accounts of God. For you are God's steward. Therefore, you are obliged to keep the accounts in such a way as to feed the poor and the orphans, if there is any surplus. After all, God is their Father and nurturer, and you are administering their goods. If there is no surplus, you should do what you can to make one. Otherwise, you are not keeping the accounts of the church but only taking care of yourself. If that is what you are doing, then you are not keeping the accounts for God but for the devil. Do everything, then, according to God and you shall find your reward in him.

Prayer and fasting

838. *Question.* Father, I try to fast each day from morning until evening. Tell me whether this is good, and whether I should pray before I do anything.

Response by Barsanuphius

As for fasting, examine your heart closely in order to see whether it is deceived by vainglory. If not, then examine it again, to see whether this fasting renders you weaker and forgetful in matters; for such weakness is not beneficial. If you are not harmed in this way as well, then your fasting is good. Prayer is light, and every Christian should pray before doing anything, especially if one is a priest of God.

The task of a bishop

844. Response by the same Great Old Man to the bishop of the city, who asked him to show him what he should do, as well as to pray for the people who were afflicted on account of the impending wrath.

Your holiness should suffer excessively with those who are afflicted. For this is the task of a spiritual father and teacher. Moreover, a good shepherd cares for and is vigilant over his sheep. Therefore, train the people to cooperate with the supplication and prayer offered for its sake; for in this way, they shall be able to achieve great things, according to the Lord's commandment.

On giving advice to a bishop

845. A Christ-loving layperson[71] asked the Other Old Man. Is it good for me to suggest to the lord bishop whatever I feel is beneficial for him?

Response by John

This is a good thing, and it is proper for a love that is according to God. Hold your heart in purity before God, and this will not cause you harm. Now, having your heart in purity means not saying anything against anyone out of vengeance, but only for the sake of good itself. Therefore, do not imagine that such a thing is slander; for everything done for the sake of correction is not slander. Nothing good results from slander; whereas, in this case, the result is good. That is why it is not slander.

The key to salvation

848. *Question.*[72] What does the sentence mean: "Rejoice always; pray without ceasing; give thanks in all circumstances" (1 Thess 5.16–18)?

Response by Barsanuphius

These three things contain our entire salvation. Always rejoicing prepares the way of righteousness; for no one can truly rejoice unless one's life always appears righteous. Praying without ceasing is the aversion of every evil; for this allows no room for the devil to act against us. Finally, giving thanks in all circumstances is clear proof of our love for Christ. If the first two properly regulate our life, then we shall give thanks to the Lord.

[71]A pious layman.
[72]From a pious layman.

Select Bibliography

This select bibliography contains three parts:

- various editions available of the text itself;
- works dealing with the *Correspondence* or its authors; and
- general books about the region and monasticism around Palestine and Gaza.

Sources

Chitty, D. J. *Barsanuphius and John: Questions and Answers*, partial critical edition of the Greek text with English translation, in *Patrologia Orietalis* XXXI, 3 (Paris, 1966), 445–616.

Migne, J.-P. Barsanuphius, *Doctrina [Teaching on Origen, Evagrius and Didymus]*, in *Patrologia Graeca*, volume 86: i, 891–902; and Dorotheus, *Questions and Answers* [incorporated among his *Instructions*], in volume 88: 1811–1822.

Nikodemus of Mt. Athos, Βίβλος ψυχωφελεστάτη περιέχουσα ἀποκρίσεις διαφόροις ὑποθέσεσιν ἀνηκούσαις, συγγραφεῖσὰ μεν παρὰ τῶν ὁσίων καὶ θεοφόρων πατέρων ἡμῶν Βαρσανουφίου καὶ Ἰωάννου, ἐπιμελῶς δὲ διορθωθεῖσα καὶ τῇ τῶν ὁσίων βιογραφίᾳ, καὶ πλατυτάτῳ πίνακι πλουτισθεῖσα παρὰ τοῦ ἐν μοναχοῖς ἐλαχίστου Νικοδήμου τοῦ ἁγιορείτου. (Venice, 1816). Also contains a substantial introduction by Nikodemus himself.

Regnault, L. *Barsanuphe et Jean de Gaza: Correspondance*, volumes I-III, in *Sources Chrétiennes* 426–7, 450–1, and 468 (Paris, 1997–2002). Critical text, notes and index by F. Neyt and P. de Angelis-Noah.

Regnault, L. Lemaire, Ph. and Ottier, B. *Barsanuphe et Jean de Gaza: Correspondance*, complete translation from the Greek and Georgian (Sable-sur-Sarthe: Abbaye de Solesmes, 1971).

Rose, S. (ed.), *Saints Barsanuphius and John: Guidance toward Spiritual Life. Answers to the Questions of Disciples* (Platina, CA: St. Herman of Alaska Brotherhood, 1990). Partial English translation from the Russian edition (Moscow, 1855).

Schoinas, S. (ed.), βίβλος ψυχωφελεστάτη . . . Βαρσανουφίου καὶ Ἰωάννου [as above in the book by Nikodemus: "Most edifying book, containing responses on various matters written by our holy and God-bearing Fathers Barsanuphius and John."] (Volos, 1960).

Barsanuphius and John

Binns, J. *Ascetics and Ambassadors of Christ: The Monasteries of Palestine 314–631* (Oxford: Oxford University Press, 1994).

Brown, P. *The Body and Society. Men, Women and Sexual Renunciation in Early Christianity* (New York: Columbia University Press, 1988).

Chitty, D. *The Desert a City: An Introduction to the Study of Egyptian and Palestinian Monasticism under the Christian Empire* (Oxford: Blackwells, 1966; reprinted: Crestwood, NY: St. Vladimir's Seminary Press, 1995)

Hausherr, I. *Direction spirituelle en Orient antrefois* (Rome, 1955). See also the English translation: *Spiritual Direction in the Early Christian East* (Kalamazoo, MI: Cistercian Publications, 1990).

Hevelone Harper, J. L. *Letters to the Great Old Man: Monks, Laity, and Spiritual Authority in Sixth-Century Gaza* (Princeton University: PhD. Dissertation, 2000).

The Lives of the Saints of the Holy Land and the Sinai Desert, translation from the *Great Synaxaristes* (Bueno Vista, CO: Holy Apostles Convent, 1988), 94–100.

Neyt, F. *Les Lettres à Dorothée dans la Correspondance de Barsanuphe et de Jean de Gaza* (Louvain: PhD. Dissertation, 1969).

Neyt, F. "Un Type d'Autorité Charismatique," *Byzantion* 44 (1974): fasc. 2, 343–361. Also appeared in English as "A Form of Charismatic Authority," *Eastern Churches Review* 6 (1974): 52–65.

Noah (de Angelis-), F. "La Méditation de Barsanuphe sur la Lettre *êta,*" *Byzantion* 53 (1983): fasc. 2, 494–506.

Perrone, L. *La Chiesa di Palestina e le Controversie Cristologiche: dal Concilio di Efeso (431) al Secondo Concilio di Constantinopoli* (Brescia: Paideia, 1980).

Rapp, C. " 'For next to God, you are my salvation': Reflections on the Rise of the Holy Man in Late Antiquity," in J. Howard-Johnston and P. A. Hayward, eds., *Essays on the Contribution of Peter Brown* (Oxford: Oxford University Press, 1999), 63–81.

Regnault, L. "Théologie de la Vie Monastique selon Barsanuphe et Dorothée," in *Théologie de la Vie Monastique: Etudes sur le Tradition Patristique* (Aubier, 1961), 315–322.

Vailhé, S. "Jean le Prophète et Séridos," *Echos d'Orient* 8 (1905): 154–160.

Vailhé, S. "Les Lettres Spirituelles de Jean et de Barsanuphe," *Echos d'Orient* 7 (1904): 268–276.

Vailhé, S. "Saint Barsanuphe," *Echos d'Orient* 8 (1905): 14–25.

Vamvakas, D. Τὸ ἐν παντὶ εὐχαριστεῖν τῶν ὁσίων καὶ θεοφόρων πατέρων ἡμῶν Βαρσανουφίου καὶ Ἰωάννου (Hagion Oros, Karyai, 1991).

General References

Aharoni, Y. *The Land of the Bible*, rev. edn. (Philadelphia, 1979).

Avi-Yonah, M. *The Madeba Mosaic Map* (Jerusalem, 1954).

Brown, P. "The Rise and Function of the Holy Man in Late Antiquity," *Journal of Religious Studies* 61 (1971): 80–101. Revised in P. Brown, *Society and the Holy in Late Antiquity* (Berkeley, CA: University of California Press, 1982).

Downey, G. *Gaza in the Early Sixth Century* (Norman, Oklahoma, 1963).

Glucker, C. A. M. *The City of Gaza in the Roman and Byzantine Periods*, BAR International Series 325 (Oxford, 1987).

Guillaumont, A. *Aux Origines de Monachisme Chrétien*, coll. *Spiritualité orientale* (Bellefontaine, 1979).

Hirschfeld, Y. *The Judean Desert Monasteries in the Byzantine Period* (New Haven: Princeton University Press, 1992).

Jones, A. M. H. *Cities of the Eastern Roman Provinces*, 2nd rev. edn. (Oxford, 1971).

Regnault, L. "Les Apophtegmes des Pères en Palestine aux Ve et Ve siècles,"
    Irénikon 54 (1981): 320–330. Later appeared as, L. Regnault, *Les Pères du
    Désert à travers leurs Apophtegmes* (Sable-sur-Sarthe: Abbaye de
    Solesmes, 1987), 73–83.

Vailhé, S. "Saint Dorothée et Saint Zosime," *Echos d' Orient* 4 (1901): 359–363.

Vailhé, S. "Un Mystique Monophysite, le moine Isaie," *Echos d' Orient* 9
    (1906): 81–91.

Van Parys, M. "Abba Silvain et ses Disciples," *Irénikon* 61 (1988): 315–330.

Index of Topics

(Please note: numbers listed refer to the letter number)

205

Index of Titles

(Please note: numbers listed refer to the page number)

Numerical Index

(Please note: numbered letters on left; page numbers on right)

EGYPT, SINAI & SOUTHERN PALESTINE

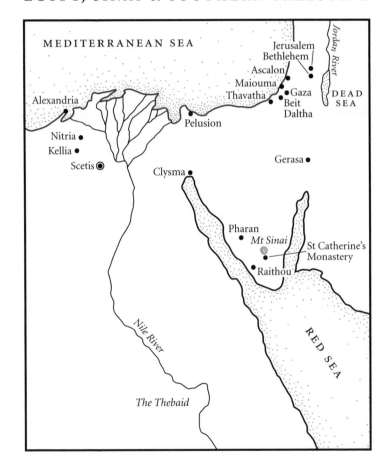